UNIVERSITY OF NORTH CAROLINA
STUDIES IN THE ROMANCE LANGUAGES AND LITERATURES
Number 63

THE ROMANCE OF FLOIRE AND BLANCHEFLEUR

Published with the aid of the

CHARLES PHELPS TAFT MEMORIAL FUND
UNIVERSITY OF CINCINNATI

THE ROMANCE OF FLOIRE
AND BLANCHEFLEUR

A FRENCH IDYLLIC POEM OF THE
TWELFTH CENTURY

TRANSLATED INTO ENGLISH VERSE

BY

MERTON JEROME HUBERT

CHAPEL HILL

THE UNIVERSITY OF NORTH CAROLINA PRESS

PRINTED IN SPAIN

DEPÓSITO LEGAL: V. 2.176 - 1966

ARTES GRÁFICAS SOLER, S. A. - VALENCIA - 1966

To Doris Ransom

TABLE OF CONTENTS

FOREWORD

I wish to thank the staff of the University of Cincinnati Library for kindness and patience in the face of what were perhaps unreasonable requests for help in the preparation of this book. The late Professor Edward B. Ham, of California has contributed numerous useful suggestions, both to this work and many others. I am under great obligation to Mrs. Grace Sales for typing and retyping the manuscript and for helping with the Index.

Above all I am indebted to the administration of the Charles Phelps Taft Memorial Fund, who continue so faithfully to carry out Mrs. Taft's desire to foster the study of the humanities.

M. J. H.

April 1966.

INTRODUCTION

1. LE ROMAN IDYLLIQUE

As the popularity of the Old French chansons de geste waned at the end of the twelfth century, a new literary genre — or genres — arose to meet the aesthetic tastes of a newer generation. Mediaeval man, largely under the influence of mediaeval woman, was growing more refined, more elegant, and more sophisticated, and less easily satisfied with sanguinary tales of the moving accident on flood and field. The crusades had given western Europe something of an acquaintance with the culture of the orient. The Provençal writers had provided examples of emotional subtlety, not to mention what is now described as gracious living. Their influence spread among the aristocratic people who could afford this gracious living along with the measure of luxury provided by their wealth and social position. It is only fair to add that Charlemagne and his peers, William of Orange and his nephews, and the whole host of blood-thirsty bickering barons continued to charm the populace.

Scholars have applied to the newer verse fiction a variety of names: romans d'aventure, romans bretons, romans de chevalerie, romans courtois. None of these terms is perfectly satisfactory, chiefly because the poems differ among themselves in tone, style and purport. Many a romance of adventure shows no trace of Breton influence, while there are courtly romances that lack the element of adventure. Mme Myrrha Lot-Borodine applies the term "roman idyllique" to a group of narratives which would be ill described by any of the other phrases.

It is to this group that the poem here presented belongs, and I can not hope to improve on her description of the type. Essentially they are stories of love, and always of youthful love. The prototype is *Daphnis and Chloe*. It is tempting to say that the twentieth century version expresses itself in the succinct phrase: "Boy meets girl, boy loses girl, boy finds girl", a standard and apparently inexhaustible formula. That formula, however, gives only a partial and misleading description. The roman idyllique developed in a narrower frame and with certain highly specialized qualities. Its essential characteristic perhaps is the unsophisticated, innocent, and artless nature of the love affair. The love is not the ferocious fatality of the ancients: Vénus toute entière à sa proie attachée. Neither is it the worldly, experienced, self-conscious love of the mature mediaeval man or woman, the courtly folk who could with real or mock seriousness debate the intricate moral problems with which civilization has complicated sexual life and produced such a fascinating and varied literature. Our two protagonists, Floire and Blanchefleur, had read Ovid when they were about ten years old, so far as one can judge: one wonders how much of him they understood. One wonders how much they would have understood of the intricate dogmas set forth by André le Chapelain in his famous treatise. Their relation is quite different: it is young love, the tender, dawning affection of two young people that Marivaux was later to portray so skillfully. It is a product of instinct, adolescence, propinquity and — so the poet assures us — of beauty, yet for all that it has the same sort of irresistible power as the curse that Aphrodite set upon Phèdre. The young Floire, little more than a child, is so wrapped up in his love that nothing else in the world has any importance in his eyes. If Blanchefleur is dead, as his parents assure him, and he can not hope to have her for his own, he craves only for death; only the intervention of his anguished mother prevents his suicide. Aucassin, his spiritual brother, displays like indifference to parental authority, worldly welfare, family pride, indeed everything that is not Nicolette. He will have Nicolette or nothing.

These characters are naïve, spontaneous, healthy and young: They fall in love as naturally as they breathe. The elaborate complications of courtly love, with its intricate code of controlled emotions and prescribed behavior, would have bewildered them, — as indeed they sometimes bewilder us. They obey the dictates of their hearts and ignore everything else.

The question naturally arises: How do these simple innocents behave in the face of opposition, frustration, and the crude realities of everyday existence, not to mention parental hostility? The answer might be that they suffer, they despair, they wail like the children they really are, yet they do not abandon their ideals, — or if you prefer, their illusions. Sometimes they take action. Nicolette escapes from prison, and takes to the woods. Floire defies his father's will and sets out to recover his loved one. But they do not give up their love. They take action merely to bring it to fruition. If such action were not necessary, they would be quite content to spend their lives in amorous delight.

Perhaps the most notable characteristic of these idyllic tales is the happy ending. This is de rigueur. The wheel of Fortune, so frequently evoked and described at length in mediaeval literature, may inflict on the hero and heroine any number of sorrows, mishaps, discomforts and miseries, but not tragedy nor disaster. Before the story ends, the lovers will be reunited, the marriage will be solemnized, parents will conveniently die so that a glittering heritage of wealth, nobility and dignity may fall into the laps of the younger generation, and all will presumably be for the best in the best of all possible worlds.

It should be added too that the genre is thoroughly aristocratic, both in the audience for which it is destined and in the cast of characters who perform. The hero or heroine may appear to be a foundling, a slave, a hapless prisoner, but it is certain that before the story ends the truth will out and the supposed underling will prove to be a prince or princess whom the wheel of Fortune has temporarily cast into the depths. There are occasional glimpses of the lower orders, such as the vivid and touching episode of Aucassin's encounter with the poor peasant who has lost his ox, but they are incidental. The lord and lady, disguised though they may be, hold the center of the stage.

So too with the audience. It would no doubt be a great oversimplification to say that the stories of battle, bloodshed and violent action, of motivated or unmotivated clash of arms, appealed only to the populace, a populace untrained and uncultivated and insensible of the more delicate and subtle aspects of life. The taste for gore is not limited to the peasantry. Nevertheless, it seems quite clear that the better-educated nobleman, and particularly the noblewoman, had more appreciation of subtleties and delicacies than did the tiller of the soil, — or the bourgeois either, for that matter.

THE MANUSCRIPTS OF FLOIRE AND BLANCHEFLEUR

This observation leads one to the fact that two different versions of *Floire and Blanchefleur* have survived in Old French, and that they appeal to two quite different audiences. One is preserved in three MSS, all in the Bibliothèque Nationale, and a fragment of a fourth in the Bibliothèque Palatine at the Vatican. The other is represented by a single MS in the Bibliothèque Nationale.

The first, probably the older, version is sometimes referred to as the aristocratic version of the story. It has been published by several editors, [1] none of whose work has completely satisfied scholarly critics. The present translation is based on the 1956 edition of Margaret Pelan, with due account taken of improvements suggested by reviewers. Edmond Faral published in 1934 a phototypic reproduction of MS 19152, Fonds Français, which contains the second version. [2] Both versions were transcribed and printed by Édélestand du Méril (Paris 1856) and by Felicitas Krüger (Berlin 1938). Except for Margaret Pelan, all editors of the first version have preferred to use the MS known as A. Margaret Pelan based her text on MS B for reasons which she explains.

The second version, a trifle longer than the first, is called popular because of its inclusion of various incidents that seem designed to please the clientele that still delighted in accounts of warfare and the modified form of warfare called tournaments. They detract from rather than add to the story, and show little originality and less art. By contrast, the older version does not contain a single tournament or armed conflict except for the raid on Christian territory with which the poem begins. This was necessary in order to explain the presence of Blanchefleur's mother as a slave at the Saracen court:

---

[1] See Bibliography.

[2] Faral's comment is pertinent: "La seconde version est un remaniement de la première, accommodé au goût d'un auditoire plus raffiné. On l'appelle habituellement 'la version des jongleurs' ou 'version populaire' par opposition à la première, la 'version aristocratique'. Op cit., pp. 47-8.

the poet does not dwell upon it with relish, indeed he gives the feeling that he is playing it down and hurrying on to his main theme which is a love story.

Another feature of the second version that deserves to be noted is the attitude of the writer toward the Saracens. [3] The authors of the chansons de geste had regularly viewed Islam as the great enemy, and described the Moslems in anything but flattering terms: they are foes of the Christian faith, bent on the extermination or the enslavement of adherents of the true religion of western Europe. They appear as savage, brutal, treacherous and menacing. Though their great wave of conquest had been halted, and the Crusades had carried on an effective counter-attack, they still held Spain, and the threat of the Moors still hung over Christianity.

None of this hostility appears in *Floire and Blanchefleur*, first version. Here they are neither better nor worse than the Christians. In fact, Floire's father, the Saracen king, consults his wife on all important decisions and allows himself to be guided by her advice, in a fashion far more suggestive of the traditional modern French bourgeois than of the traditional Moslem tyrant. His queen too is a fitting consort for him, kind-hearted but shrewd and practical, and if her worldly wisdom produces unhappy results, it is only fair to observe that she is trying to make the best of a bad situation.

FLOIRE AND BLANCHEFLEUR AS A WORK OF ART

The description of the *roman idyllique* is a fair though not complete description of *Floire and Blanchefleur*, which is probably the earliest of those that have been preserved. It has its defects, some of which are common to almost all mediaeval literature. Most of its weaknesses, however, are counterbalanced by the fact that its author — of whom we know nothing beyond what we can deduce from his text — possessed a considerable gift for telling a story. It moves smoothly and rapidly, interrupted only at rare intervals by the overdeveloped descriptive passages that so many poets of the Middle Ages could not resist the temptation to introduce. Even these purple patches have a peculiar intangible charm of their own, though one

[3]   See W. W. Comfort in *Dublin Review*, Vol. 149 (July 1911), pp. 23-49.

is sometimes well-advised not to examine them too closely. Blanche-
fleur's supposed tomb, for instance, elaborately contrived, decorated
and landscaped in practically no time at all, is fascinating, for all
the strain it puts on our credulity. And what shall we say of the
marvelous cup, adorned with the complete history of the Trojan war,
which Aeneas carried away with him when he took off for the West?
We are not told how he managed to get it completed in time. We
may also be amused by the happy series of coincidences that com-
bine to guide the questing Floire so conveniently and so accurately
in his search for his lost sweetheart.

I have just used the word 'amused.' This word perhaps describes
as well as any the reaction which the story of *Floire and Blanche-
fleur* is likely to produce on a reader. It is hard to take the vicissi-
tudes of the lovers too seriously: one knows that boy will recover
girl, that the obstacles to felicity will vanish, the threatened disasters
be averted. In fact, I am inclined to suspect that the writer was aware
of this. He undoubtedly had a sense of humor. The bumbling king,
ferocious in a raiding expedition, but a figure of comedy in his
domestic affairs, is not quite ridiculous but very nearly so. The
porter of the emir's tower, whose greed almost seals his doom and
who is quite aware of his weakness, will provoke a smile though
not a burst of laughter. And the emir himself, who goes through
an elaborate ritual of leaving to chance the choice of a wife for
each new year, but carefully arranges — 'by necromancy' — to have
the magic leaf fall upon a girl whom he has singled out beforehand!
Is he not a comic figure? Then there is the scene in which Floire,
transported into his sweetheart's room concealed in a huge basket
of roses, emerges to find he is in the wrong room and is looking
at a girl he has never seen before. This could have been written for
a late nineteenth century farce. I do not wish to overemphasize this
aspect of the poet's talent, but rather to suggest that he has a certain
lightness of touch and a delicate gaiety of spirit that have not been
blurred by the passage of time.

Incidentally, the later popular version provides a striking con-
trast. Whether it is a rewriting of the aristocratic version or whether
the two derive from some lost original, the author of the popular
version completely lacks any of these engaging qualities. He tells
his story clumsily, brings in much extraneous material, glosses over
essential features of the narrative, and manages to communicate to

the light tale of love an atmosphere of grim and ponderous sobriety. Version I is the work of an artist, — a minor artist perhaps, but still an artist. Version II was written by a journeyman.

Date and Sources of Floire and Blanchefleur

Nowhere in our story does the author give his name, nor does any other document provide us with even a trace of evidence that would identify him. We do, however, know something about the date when he lived and wrote. His obvious acquaintance with the *Roman d'Enéas* which is usually dated about 1155, establishes that year as the earliest possible one. There is some evidence that he had completed it by 1170, which is the established date of a Low-German adaptation of the tale. The evidence is not wholly conclusive, since the Low-German poem might conceivably have its origin in an earlier French poem which we no longer possess. [4] The style of our poem, however, suggests that it was composed not much if at all later than 1170, and for lack of anything more precise we may well accept the period 1155-1170 as probable.

Scholars naturally have hunted far and wide for the sources of the story. The oriental or pseudo-oriental setting and the fact that most of the characters are presented as Moslems [5] have focussed attention on eastern literature. Perhaps it is appropriate to point out that except for Babylon — which of course is Cairo — the geography of the poem is very perplexing, or would be if one did not simply accept it as fanciful. The Saracen king, setting forth on his raid on Christian territory, sails from Spain to Galicia; when he returns laden with loot, he returns to Naples, which Pelan suggests may be Noples, a spot whose existence may be purely literary. [6] It might also be Naplouse, which has the merit of existing. Floire is sent, ostensibly to study, to Montoire, which is equally vague. When he later takes ship in search of Blanchefleur, his sea-voyage terminates at Bauduc, of which we learn that it is perched on a cliff high above

---

[4] See Du Méril, pp. xxviii, ff.

[5] Though one of the emir's retainers is referred to as a "bishop" (line 2808).

[6] Op. cit., p. 141.

the water, and that it is four days' journey from Babylon. On the third day the road crosses a "braz de mer" — what I dare say we should now call an inlet — named Frelle, guarded by a stronghold called Montfelix. I have been unable to identify any of these places. And even Cairo has its confusing aspects, for it is fringed by the Euphrates, "one of the rivers of paradise." I think one may fairly describe the topography as imaginary, created by the poet out of names he had heard or read.

I am disposed to believe that the plot too came from the imagination of the French poet. To be sure there are passages where the influence of the *Roman d'Eneas* is apparent. And one or another feature of the tale can be found in various works to which the writer might just conceivably have had access. Evidence has been cited to demonstrate that he could have derived this or that from stories existing in Byzantine literature, in Persian literature and in Arabic literature. The evidence seems to me far too tenuous to justify a conclusion in any one of these surmises. J. Reinhold, who has devoted an article and a thesis to *Floire and Blanchefleur,* [7] finds possible sources in Apuleius' story of Cupid and Psyche, in the *Golden Ass.* He also discovers possibilities in the *Book of Esther.* These seem to me quite as conjectural as any of the others. In fact, I can see no reason for assuming that *Floire and Blanchefleur* is anything more than the free creation of the French poet who wrote it, always with the proviso that there may have existed a version prior to the one we have.

This view was expressed, albeit with a certain mild scholarly reluctance, by G. Lozinski: "En la relisant, on est même tenté de se demander si elle n'est pas née tout simplement dans le cerveau d'un Français qui l'aurait agrémentée de quelques traits de "turquerie élémentaire'." [8] After all, new stories and fresh plots are invented and written every day in the twentieth century. Conceding that mediaeval writers had an exaggerated veneration for the written word, and loved to derive their material from the documents of the past which they cited with such relish, it still seems to me unjustified to assume that the creative gift should have gone into complete eclipse during the middle ages.

---

[7] Floire et Blanchefleur, Étude de littérature comparée (Paris, 1906).
[8] Litteraturblatt für Germanische und Romanische Philologie, 1942-3, p. 39.

LATER FORTUNES OF FLOIRE ET BLANCHEFLEUR

Though the origin of our story may be difficult to determine with any degree of precision, its popularity with mediaeval readers would be hard to dispute. Perhaps popularity is not the right word. Perhaps one might more properly say that the names of the two lovers became a legend, a sort of symbol of faithful and unswerving devotion. One finds them cited, over and over again, along with Tristan and Iseult, and Lancelot and Guinevere, as perfect examples of those who loved and suffered for their love, very much as Romeo and Juliet are cited in later days. A few quotations may be appropriate. Karl Bartsch prints an *aubade* of the 12th century containing these lines:

> D'un doux lai d'amor
> De Blancheflor,
> Compains, vos chanteroie, [9]

as well as a pastourelle which begins:

> "Floires revient seus de Montoire
> Cui fins amors a pris an laz, [10]

and continues with the account of Floire's grief at the supposed death of his sweetheart.

In the south the Countess Beatriz de Dia, one of the rare women troubadours, sings of her lover:

> Car plus m'en suis abellida
> No fez Floris de Blancheflor, [11]

and a thirteenth century aubade of Uc de la Bacalaria also refers to them. Flamenca, in the same century, tests the carrying-power of her voice by reading to her handmaidens a passage from the Romance of Blanchefleur — a natural choice, we may conclude,

---

[9] *Chrestomathie de l'ancien Français* (Leipzig 1927, 12th ed.), p. 168.
[10] *Altfranzösische Romanzen und Pastourellen* (Leipzig 1870, p. 15.
[11] Hill and Bergin: *Anthology of the Provençal Troubadours*, (New Haven 1941), p. 53.

for she too was a prisoner in a high tower. Examples of this sort could be multiplied, ranging from Portugal to Greece; Crescini and DuMéril have noted many of them. [12] Maurice Delbouille has found what he believes to be definite indications of the influence of *Floire et Blanchefleur* in other poems of the later twelfth and early thirteenth centuries, notably the *Eracle* of Gautier d'Arras, the *Lanval* and *Guigemar* of Marie de France, the early *Tristan* of Thomas, and the *Erec et Enide* of Chrétien de Troyes. [13] Miss Pelan observes that the parallels he cites to prove his point seem less convincing to her than they do to Delbouille. [14] I entirely agree with her.

Adaptations, translations, and more or less altered retellings of the tale appeared in numerous languages of both the north and south of Europe, and continued to appear, well into the period of the Renaissance. DuMéril, in his long introduction, has given a carefully studied — through not always completely lucid — account of these versions and their variations. To his work and that of Crescini we refer the reader who may wish to follow in detail the progress of the story. We can note here only a few of the versions. Among the earliest and best known is perhaps the Middle High German of Konrad Fleck, [15] entitled *Floire und Blanschesflur,* which dates from the beginning of the thirteenth century. This is followed by translations or adaptations in Flemish, Czech, the various Scandinavian tongues (including Icelandic), Middle English, Italian, Spanish and Yiddish. Merely to enumerate them all would unduly prolong this introduction, but one must mention that Boccaccio used the story as the basis for his *Filocolo*. A modern French version was published in 1929. [16]

The lack of any translation in modern English may perhaps justify the present volume, whose preparation has really been a labor of love.

---

[12]   Crescini, Vincenzo: *Il Cantare di Fiorio e Biancafiore* (Bologna 1889 and 1899).

[13]   Delbouille, Maurice: A propos de la patrie et de la date de *Floire et Blanchefleur,* in Mélanges de linguistique et de littérature romanes offerts à Mario Roques (Paris 1952), pp. 53-99.

[14]   Op. cit., p. xxiii.

[15]   Sommer, Emil.: Floire und Blanschesflur, eine Erzahlung von Konrad Fleck. Quadlinburg and Leipzig, 1846.

[16]   Marchand, J.: La Légende de Floire et Blanchefleur (renouvellement). Paris 1929.

FLOIRE AND BLANCHEFLEUR

A NOBLE LINEAGE

1   Hear, lords, hear lovers all, all those
Who bear the burden of love's woes;
Maidens and knights, hark to my words,
4   You gentle damsels and young lords.
If you will hear my tale, you may
Learn many things about Love's way.
'Tis of the young Prince Floire I tell
8   And Blanchefleur the good demoiselle.
'Twas Bertha Broadfoot, born of them,
Who in France wore the queen's diadem
As noble Pepin's queen. In turn
12   To them the great King Charles was born.
Bertha was dam of Charlemagne
Who was to rule o'er France and Maine.
A paynim king engenderèd
16   Her father Floire, as I have said;
While Blanchefleur, she whom Floire adored,
Was fathered by a Christian lord.
Floire came of paynim lineage,
20   Blanchefleur of Christian parentage.
Then, Floire was baptized and became
Christian to please Blanchefleur his dame.
On the same night begotten, they
24   Were both born on the selfsame day.
Once baptized Christian, Floire grew great
In wealth and land and high estate:

He became King of Hungary
28   And held Bulgaria's sovereignty.
His uncle who was ruler there
Had died leaving no other heir,
And since Floire was his sister's son
32   He thus inherited the throne.

THE TELLING OF THE TALE

I take my story now in hand
And tell it fitly as I planned.
One Friday, after my repast
36   Was done, into a room I passed
Where I would find, as I knew well
Many a comely demoiselle,
And in this room there was a bed
40   On which a rich silk cloth was spread
With a gay hem of red and azure
And exquisite beyond all measure,
The silk of wondrous quality;
44   No finer silk from Thessaly
E'er came. And thereupon I sat
Listening to the damsels' chat.
They were two sisters, and the theme
48   That they discussed was love, 'twould seem.
The elder to her sister told
A love-tale of the days of old
About a noble youth and maid
52   Two hundred years ago, she said.
She had it from a clerk who took
The story from a written book.
In seemly fashion she began
56   And this is how the story ran:

A MOSLEM RAID IN CHRISTIAN LAND

A king one day set forth from Spain
With many fine knights in his train.

Boarding their ships, the sea they crossed
60 And landed on Galicia's coast.
This paynim king, Fenix by name,
Into the Christian country came
To burn the towns to ashes, plunder,
64 Rob, and despoil, and rip asunder.
A whole month and two weeks beside,
The king ravaged the land. He'd ride
Forth each day with his knights. The king
68 Made no end of his pillaging.
He spoiled the towns, he sacked and harried,
And to the ships his loot he carried.
For thirty leagues from the shore-line
72 He left no trace of herd nor kine,
Nor did castle nor wood remain
Standing. The peasant sought in vain
His ox. The land was all destroyed,
76 While the paynim were overjoyed.
At last the king, wishing to fare
Homeward, gave orders to prepare
His ships. He summoned to him then
80 Some forty of his noblemen.

A PARTING FORAY

"Arm yourselves, my lords," he commands,
"Leave ship-loading to other hands.
Take to the high roads and waylay
84 Such pilgrims as may come your way."
Into the country forth they go
And scan the plain stretching below.
From their high point the knights descried
68 Pilgrims scaling the mountain-side.
Swooping down on them, they attack
These pilgrims, who could not fight back,
And most of whom, all shuddering
92 With fear, surrendered everything.
Among them there was a French knight,

Urbane and noble and upright:
My Lord Saint James's shrine he sought.
96   With him his daughter he had brought:
She, before leaving home, had made
Vows to the saint. These she obeyed.
'Twas for her husband who had died
100   And whose child she now bore inside
Her womb. Bravely the good knight fought.
To capture him alive was not
Their aim. They slaughtered him, in short,
104   And dragged the bride off to the port
And gave her to king Fenix. He
Observed her very searchingly.

A LOVELY CAPTIVE IS BROUGHT HOME

He judged from looking at her face
108   That she was of a noble race,
Deciding, should nought intervene,
That he would give her to the queen
Who had requested such a maid,
112   Before he set forth on this raid.
Thereupon they all went aboard
Their ships, raised sails that had been lowered,
And with a steady favoring breeze
116   Sailed home contented and at ease.
In less than two days the wind bore
Them without mishap to their shore.
They disembarked upon the strand,
120   The king and his triumphant band.
To Naples, that fair town, report
Came that the ships were safe in port
As messengers sped on to bring
124   The gladsome news about the king.
So the townsfolk came forth to meet him
And with the greatest pleasure greet him.
They're glad too that their friends have come
128   Back safe and unharmed to their home.

SHE IS GIVEN TO THE QUEEN

The king entered his city, then
Summoned his knights and gentlemen.
Being noble, generously he shared
132   The loot with all those who had fared
With him. And to the queen as well
He gave the lovely demoiselle.
The queen, charmed, made all haste to give
136   Her a fine room in which to live;
She let her keep her faith with honor
And lavished kindnesses upon her.
The girl, gentle and cordial,
140   Won warm affection from all.
In turn she served the queen as one
To whom she owed devotion.
The queen was sewing one day on
144   Her husband's royal gonfalon,
With the girl working by her side,
When all at once the queen espied
The Christian all atremble, turning
148   Pale, now shivering, now burning,
Holding her belly, now attacked
By pain and now by nausea racked.
The queen was certain of the source
152   Of this: she was with child of course.
She asked the girl how long ago
She got this pain that racks her so.
Learning how much time had gone by
156   Since that day, the queen made reply
That she was in the self-same state
And had been since the self-same date.
They thus could foretell easily
160   The time for their delivery.
On Palm Sunday, the story goes —
As it is told by one who knows —
The time came for them to give birth
164   And for their wombs' fruit to come forth.

FLOIRE AND BLANCHEFLEUR

Through great travail and pain they passed
Before the babes were born at last.
It was a girl the Christian had.
168   The paynim bore a little lad.
And when their mothers' pangs were eased,
The children were named for the feast.
The Christian gave her girl the name
172   Of Blanchefleur, for the day she came.
Floire was the name bestowed upon
The paynim rulers' little son.
A most profound love the king bore
176   For his son, the queen even more.
They placed him in the Christian's care —
She was kind, as they were well aware. —
She did not nurse him at the breast
180   But cared for him in all the rest.
A paynim nursed him; this was done
By rule of their religion.
The Christian reared him tenderly,
184   More than her own child. Nor did she
Within her heart distinguish clearly
Which of the two she loved more dearly.

THE BOY AND GIRL ARE REARED TOGETHER

Save only for the suckling, they
188   Took food and drink in the same way.
They slept together in one bed,
Together drank, together fed.
After five years had passed, each one
192   Was big and healthy and well-grown.
You might seek anywhere you please
Nor find a finer pair than these.
When the king saw his son in truth
196   A babe no longer, but a youth

With understanding, who'd attained
The age when his mind must be trained,
He sent to him to a teacher named
200   Gaidon, a good clerk, well acclaimed,
Of his own household and related
To him, well-bred and educated.
The king ordered his child to learn.
204   But the boy, weeping and forlorn
Replied: "But what will Blanchefleur do,
My lord? Will she not study too?
Without her I shall master nought
208   Nor learn the lessons as they're taught."
"For love of you," the king replies,
"I shall command Blanchefleur likewise
To go to school with you." The boy
212   On hearing this was filled with joy.
They go together, greatly pleased,
And their affection is increased.

THEY LEARN TOGETHER

Both learned so well and with such zest,
216   'Twas marvelous how they progressed.
The two, alike in comeliness,
Loved each other with tenderness.
And they were always in a dither
220   When separated from each other.
As soon as nature made them fit
For love, they turned their hearts to it .
And yet to learning too they turned
224   And retained everything they learned.
Authors they read and books of old,
And when they heard what Ovid told
About love's ways and how folk loved —
228   Tales which they heartily approved —
His volume whetted even more
Their wish love's country to explore,
And without let or hindrance each

232   Strove to learn all he had to teach.
        Together they read, learn, inquire,
        And to the joys of love aspire.

THEIR CHILDISH LOVE

        As they return from school, 'tis this
236   That makes them pause, embrace, and kiss,
        And walking thus together daily,
        They love each other blithely, gaily.
        Floire's father has an orchard fair:
240   Mandragora was planted there,
        With herbs and flowers of every kind
        And every color you could find
        Or think of. In the shrubs and trees
244   Birds sing sweet amorous melodies.
        The children go there every day;
        They take their ease, eat, drink, and play,
        And while the two are frolicking,
248   Above their heads the small birds sing,
        Enhancing with their melody
        The children's fun and gaiety.
        After their breakfast, all aglow
252   With pleasure, off to school they go.
        Arriving there, they eagerly
        Take their tablets of ivory
        And grave upon the wax thereof
256   Verses and letters, all of love.
        Their styluses are made of gold
        And silver. As their thoughts unfold,
        Love's greetings blossom in their words,
260   With songs of flowers and of birds.
        They crave for nothing further. Thus
        Their life is sweet and glorious.

THE KING DISAPPROVES

        In five years and a fortnight, these
264   Two studied so well that with ease

They could speak Latin, and indite
Their sentiments on parchment white
When they spoke Latin, those who heard
268 Them could not understand a word.
Observing his son and Blanchefleur,
The king knew that the boy loved her,
And he could not help but presage
272 With fear that when Floire reached the age
For marriage, 'twould be hard to break
The bond and make the lad forsake
Her. To the queen's chamber he went
276 To discuss this predicament,
Quite prepared, should the queen agree,
To have the girl slain instantly,
And then to seek out for his son
280 A wife of high position.
The queen, seeing his face, could gauge
The nature of her husband's rage.
His brow purple with sheer vexation,
284 He thus spoke forth his indignation:
"Madame, affairs are far from right:
Our son is in a pretty plight.
Unless we take steps vigorous
288 And swift, he will be lost to us."
"How?" said she. "Madame, I aver
Our son so dotes upon Blanchefleur,
Our captive's daughter, that folk say
292 His love will ne'er falter nor stray
And he will love her all his life
Nor ever take another wife.
I fear, unless we act with haste,
296 Our lineage will be debased.
"The best thing I can do," he said,
"Is promptly to cut off her head,
Find an emir's daughter, or one
300 Of royal blood, to wed my son."

THE QUEEN COUNSELS MODERATION

The queen after some cogitation
Replied with wise deliberation.
She wished to succor and support
304   The girl, yet counsel in such sort
Her lord that she would satisfy
Him and that Blanchefleur would not die:
"We must find some device, some ruse
308   To insure that our son will not lose,
For Blanchefleur's love, in rank and glory,
In honor and in territory.
If we could manage not to slay
312   The girl, but just send her away,
'Twould be a less ignoble deed."
To this the king promptly agreed:
"Madame, 'tis true beyond a doubt.
316   Now how shall we bring this about?"
"Sir," she replied, "let us send Floire
Our son to study at Montoire.
My sister, Sibyl, governs there,
320   And will be pleased to give him care.
Ceasing to see her constantly
He will forget her readily,
This Christian Blanchefleur, and will find
324   Some other love to fill his mind.
Gaidon must feign that he is ill
And so unable to fulfil
His task. We'll soothe the boy's concern
328   By saying he's been sent to learn.
If his teacher were well and fit
No doubt he'd be aware of it:
People who are in love are quick
332   To guess what's back of guile and trick.
He'll be upset, and seriously:
He'll want her to accompany
Him. Thus her mother too must feign
336   Illness, and the girl must remain

As nurse to care for her and tend her.
You'll swear that two weeks hence you'll send her
There." This plan once settled on,
340 The king then summoned Floire, his son,
But set in motion first the plot
That with the queen he had worked out.

FLOIRE IS SENT AWAY TO SCHOOL

He called the young prince to him and
344 Imparted to him his command.
Young Floire responded in dismay:
"My lord, have mercy on me, pray. "
"Son, you'll obey the command I give:
348 It is your sire's prerogative."
"But, sire, how can I bid adieu
To Blanchefleur and my tutor too?
Let her accompany me, please."
352 The king then readily agrees,
That though her dam die or recover,
She'll join him ere a fortnight's over.
Reluctant, but with no excuse
356 To give, the boy can not refuse.
The king called the seneschal, had
The horses saddled for the lad,
Providing him with such a train
360 As a king's son ought to maintain.
Thus convoyed, to Montoire he went,
A castle most magnificent,
And therein Duke Jorran with joy
364 Hospitably received the boy,
His aunt likewise. The boy professed
A total lack of interest.

FLOIRE IS WRETCHED WITHOUT BLANCHEFLEUR

Lacking Blanchefleur, he could not bring
368 Himself to care for anything.

Though Sibyl took him hopefully
To meet the damsels of the city,
Trying to make the youth forget
372   Blanchefleur for some maid newly met,
He heard not, saw not, nor expressed
The slightest sign of interest.
He learned nothing from what he heard:
376   With sorrow all his thought was blurred.
Love has assailed him fore and aft,
Setting within his heart a graft
Which grew apace and blossomed well
380   In flowers of such delightful smell
That all joys save this were abated:
The fruit of this graft he awaited ...
....
But the time stretched out very long,
384   It seemed, ere ripe fruit would appear
Thereon and Blanchefleur would lie near
Him, kiss him, nestle by his side,
And thus the ripened fruit provide.
388   Morose, dejected, Floire attended
Until the fortnight should be ended.
When she came not, he realized
He had been hoaxed and victimized.
392   He was alarmed and filled with dread,
Suspecting that she might be dead;
He ate not, slept not, seemed quite numb.
His aunt feared that he might succumb.
396   He would not touch a thing to drink,
Wept constantly, appeared to shrink
From all laughter or merriment.
His heart torn and his spirit rent.

A NEW PLAN IS DEVISED BY HIS PARENTS

400   The king, learning this situation,
Was filled with grief and irritation,
Gave him leave to return, and then
In rage summoned the queen again.

404   Said he: "These tidings that I learn
      Have done the damsel an ill turn
      She may perhaps, by necromancy,
      Once more bewitch my young son's fancy.
408   Send her to me without delay.
      I'll have her head cut off straightway.
      He'll see she's dead, and being young
      He will forget her before long."
412   "My fair dear lord," the queen replies,
      "In God's name, heed what I advise.
      This port has a profusion
      Of rich merchants from Babylon.
416   She's fair. They'll take her, never fear.
      And that will be the last you hear
      Of her. 'Twill be as if she died,
      Yet we'll commit no homicide."
420   The king gave unwilling assent.
      The maiden to the port he sent
      With a burgher of sagacity
      Who spoke several tongues fluently.
424   The king did not sell her for gain
      Or lucre that he might obtain.
      He'd give a shipful of red gold
      To have her dead rather than sold.
428   But, fearful lest he might commit
      A sin, he acquiesced in it. *

A MAGNIFICENT GOLDEN CUP

      Thirty gold marks, of silver twenty,
      A score of silks from Boniventi,
432   Ten tunics of a rich dark blue,
      Ten eastern cloaks of varied hue,
      A rich gold cup filched from the store
      Of the mighty Roman emperor,
436   A masterpiece of handicraft.

----

   * M. Pelan says there is apparently a lacuna here in MS. There is no
verb to introduce nouns in next sentence.

From finer cup no man e'er quaffed,
A marvelous accomplishment
Of art skilled and intelligent.
440 Vulcan himself, the clever fellow, **
Wrought it most subtly in niello.
Troy and its stronghold were inlaid
Upon the brim, and he portrayed
444 The Greeks assailing from without,
Exchanging savage blow and clout;
Duke Paris too was painted there
Stealing away Helen the fair,
448 Done in enamel white, applied
As decoration on one side.
Next, how her husband, fierce and wroth,
Over the sea pursued them both;
452 How, at Agamemnon's command,
The waters by the Greeks were spanned;
Then, carved upon the lid, above,
How Venus, fair goddess of love,
456 With Pallas and with Juno came,
That Paris might judge each one's claim
To a fine apple of pure gold
Which each desired to have and hold.
460 They'd found it. Words written upon it
Said the most beautiful should own it.
This fruit to Paris they had handed
And of the young man had demanded
464 That he choose her whose supreme beauty
Earned it. He would not shirk this duty.
Each one offers rich recompense
If he'll give her the preference.
468 Juno, wealth and prosperity;
Pallas, noble sagacity;
While Venus promised he might have
Whatever woman he might crave.
472 The love of Paris was displayed

** Text has "Uns quens." K. Sneyders de Vogel, reviewing new edition in *Neophilologus*, 1958 (2), p. 156, says it should undoubtedly be "Vulcans," a reading which I accept as reasonable. "Uns cuens" makes little sense.

Here, and his task was well portrayed,
And in what manner he prepared
His ships as oversea he fared.
476 Atop, as on a coronet,
A carbuncle of price was set.
No cellar so distant from light,
So dim, but that the butler might
480 His finest, rarest wines descry
When guided by that lucent eye.
There was a bird above it: ne'er
Has any man seen bird more fair.
484 The gem was set inside its claw:
Never was finer. When you saw
It, you were sure, past all denying,
The creature was alive and flying.
488 King Aeneas, putting to sea
From Troy, took it with him. Then he
Bestowed the cup, in Lombardy,
On Lavinia whom he tenderly
492 Adored. And thence it was to come
To all the mighty lords of Rome,
Even Caesar. From him, we are told,
'Twas stolen by the thief who sold
496 It here. And here the purchaser
Gave it in barter for Blanchefleur.

BLANCHEFLEUR IS SOLD AS A SLAVE

He and his friends bought her and went
Their way lighthearted and content:
500 If they can get home, they've no doubt
They'll double what they have paid out.
They took ship, a fair wind prevailed
And back to their own land they sailed.
504 To Babylon these men conveyed her
Where to the emir they displayed her.
He bought her gladly, gladly paid
In fine gold seven times what she weighed.
508 Her loveliness of form and face.

Showed that she came of noble race,
And he, moved by her beauty's spell,
Ordered his men to guard her well.
512 The merchants in their turn departed,
Greatly enriched and hence light-hearted.
The king's agent likewise had paid
The king the profit he had made.
516 The queen then, after long reflection,
Spoke to the king with circumspection.
Said she: "What tale can we contrive,
When our son Floire returns, to give
520 Him? He'll ask for his friend straightway,
And then what are we going to say?
What shall we say that will avert
His dying of distressful hurt,
524 When, as he's sure to, he'll inquire
What's happened to his heart's desire?
I fear that, helpless to withstand
His grief, he'll die by his own hand."
528 "Dame," said he, "Put your mind upon
This. Comfort him. He is our son."

AN EMPTY TOMB IS PREPARED

"Indeed," said she, "I have reflected.
We'll have a noble tomb erected,
532 Of marble and of crystal, scrolled
And decked with silver and pure gold.
We'll tell him that Blanchefleur is dead:
Our son may thus be comforted."
536 "Yes," said he, "We must not delay.
Floire will arrive soon, I dare say."
They sent for master masons then,
All skillful and proficient men,
540 Who built a tomb of pulchritude
Past all that mortal eyes have viewed.
Most expertly the tomb was made,
With gold and silver-work inlaid.

544 There's no beast, no fowl of the air,
Whose image is not pictured there,
Nor any creature serpentine,
Fish from fresh water or from brine.

548 This marble tomb was carefully
Placed near a church, beneath a tree.
Goldsmiths from Friesland carved a stone
Which artfully was set thereon

552 And which was of a marble rare
And beautiful beyond compare,
Blue, yellow, black, vermilion,
Gleaming and glowing in the sun.

556 Fine Solomonic work was wrought
In subtle inlay round about. *
Silver and gold enamel brightened
Its splendor, which clear crystal heightened.

560 Above, cast in a lovely mold,
Two children's images in gold:
Statues so handsome, I surmise,
Were never seen by human eyes.

564 No likeness ever could be more
Faithful than one to young Floire bore;
The other, true to life, portrayed
The features of Blanchefleur the maid,

568 And Blanchefleur's image, with hand raised,
Held up a flower on which Floire gazed.
A rose of pure and precious gold
Before her friend she seemed to hold,

572 While to his sweetheart Floire, her lover,
A gold white lily seemed to offer.
They sat together side by side
In sweet companionship allied.

576 Upon Floire's head the dazzling rays
Of a bright carbuncle ablaze
Spread for a full league glorious light
Dispelling even the darkest night.

580 Set in the tomb's four corners there

---

* A jewelers' technique. See C. B. Davies in *Medium Aevum* **XXIX**, pp. 173-182. The term is always suggestive of great magnificence.

Were four hollow pipes placed with care,
So that one of the four winds through
One or another of them blew.
584 And then, — so were the statues placed —
One kissed the other and embraced.
By magic, seemingly, this motion
Expressed their love and their devotion,
588 As Floire to Blanchefleur seemed to say:
"Kiss me for love, sweet one, I pray."
She, kissing him, this answer gives:
"I love you more than all that lives."
592 While the wind blows upon them, this
Continues and prolongs their kiss,
And when the wind no longer blows
The two youths quietly repose
596 Gazing at each other meanwhile
With heartening and happy smile.

SURROUNDED BY TREES AND BIRDS

Above this tomb, on a high spot,
A little tree had been set out,
600 Its branches widely spread and gay
With blossoms in brilliant array:
Its boughs are always laden, bright
With flowers of gorgeous red and white.
604 Ebony is this fine tree's name.
Its wood burns not in hottest flame.
A terebinth vermilion
Grows somewhat lower, towards the sun;
608 Beneath the heavens no lovelier grows,
Fairer indeed than flowering rose.
To the left a balm-tree reared its head.
While rightward a fine chrism-tree spread
612 Its boughs. There's no fragrance on earth
Equal to that their blooms waft forth.
From one flowed chrism perpetually,
While balm dripped from the other tree.

616   Those who had set these four trees there
        To all the gods made urgent prayer,
        Prayer of such efficacity
        That the trees blossomed endlessly.
620   In blooming splendor spread the trees,
        Where birds too warbled without cease
        In melody so exquisite
        No ear e'er heard the like of it.
624   From the birds such sweet songs resound
        That their magic would have held spellbound
        Any maiden or youth in love
        Who heard these sweet airs sung above.
628   And as they listened they'd be stirred
        To deepest love by what they heard:
        Roused by the music magical,
        Into each other's arms they'd fall
632   And kiss. While hearers who loved not,
        Indeed had given love no thought,
        Were lulled by the sweet song to deep
        Prompt, quiet, and untroubled sleep.
636   The tomb that they had built was thus
        Flanked by these four miraculous
        Trees. Never was a tomb so fair
        Built for a maiden anywhere.
640   The tomb was bordered and surrounded
        With rich enamels, all around it,
        And precious jewels which possess
        A magical effectiveness:
644   Jacinth, sapphire, chalcedony,
        Emerald, sardonyx fair to see,
        And good coral and chrysolite,
        Amethyst, diamond dazzling bright,
648   And in relief are manifold
        Letters in purest Arab gold,
        Which anyone who's literate
        Can read. And this is what they state:
652   "The beautiful Blanchefleur lies here,
        She whom Floire loved and held so dear."
        The king gave orders to the queen

And to all others who had been
656   Privy to this, that they must give
Floire no inkling she was alive.
For if the young prince ever knew,
He'd have no rest, but would pursue
660   The maid, search for her far and wide,
And take her for his honored bride.
All were required to keep the youth
From any knowledge of the truth.

FLOIRE HEARS THAT HIS TRUE LOVE IS DEAD

664   But, having the king's leave to come,
Floire lingered not in coming home.
Dismounting from the horse he rode,
Into the king's great hall he strode,
666   Greeted his parents courteously,
And asked where his sweetheart might be.
He saw her not. They said nought. Worried,
Into the bed-chamber he hurried.
672   He found the maiden's mother there
And told her his mistrust and care.
"Madame, where is my friend?" he cried.
"Faith, not here, my lord," she replied.
676   "Where then?" "I know not." "Call her here."
"I can't." "You're mocking me, I fear.
"You're hiding her." "No, I protest."
"Fore God, this is a sorry jest."
680   What she must say could not be kept
From his ears. She broke down and wept,
Murmuring through her tears: "She's dead."
"Is this true?" "'Tis as I have said."
684   She said to Floire who was forlorn,
Anguished, his heart stricken and torn
By loss of her whom he so cherished:
"Sir, 'twas for love of you she perished."
688   She lied, as she was well aware,
Swearing what the king made her swear.

Floire, hearing she was dead, grew numb
And helpless; he was overcome
692   With anguish, shocked and desolate.

HE IS PROSTRATED

Upon the floor he fell prostrate.
The Christian woman, terrified
And dazed, for aid and succor cried.
696   She cried so loudly that the king
Heard her shouts, and came hurrying.
And the queen too, with shrill lament
At her son's dire predicament.
700   Three times he swooned in his distress,
Then slowly regained consciousness.
"Why then does Death forget me here
And take her whom I hold most dear?
704   Take me, Madame," he said to her,
"Take me to see her sepulchre."
His mother in grief-stricken gloom
Escorts the youth to Blanchefleur's tomb;
708   He sees the letters that declare
How young Floire loved Blanchefleur the fair.
Then three more fainting-spells eclipse
His spirit ere words pass his lips,
712   And for support he clings tight to
The tree that at the tomb-side grew,
The while, in tears and tenderness,
He speaks of Blanchefleur's loveliness:
716   "Ah Blanchefleur, you with face so bright,
On one same day we saw the light, *
Begotten the same night as well,
As we have heard our mothers tell.
720   Together we were reared and taught,
And so, it seems to me, we ought
To quit this life on the same day

---

* In Pelan's edition (1936) 11.716-17 do not rhyme. In 1956 they do.
A printer's error?

Were Death but righteous in her way.
724 Ah Blanchefleur, you with face so bright,
Though rank may seem to disunite
Us, none of your age ever could
Be so supremely fair and good.
728 Why did you die, woman most dear?
Your like will not again appear.
Such beauty none would dare essay
To tell, nor could mere words portray:
732 So hard the task that whosoever
Essayed would fail in his endeavor.
Your face, your hair, your head, — I'd call
Him wise who could describe them all.
736 Ah, glowing, tender, fresh complexion!
None e'er was born of such perfection:
Beauty's own laurel-wreath you bore
And chastity's insignia wore.
740 Humble you were and kind, indeed
Always helpful to those in need:
All, great and small, perceived so clearly
This kindness that all loved you dearly.
744 Sweet, when we learned our lessons, we
Loved each other devotedly.
Spoken in Latin, all the good
We said could not be understood.

HE UPBRAIDS DEATH

748 Ah Death! Greedy and tyrannous,
Of foul intent and envions,
You do not come at the behest
Of those who call and love you best.
752 Instead, you're perversely disposed
To seize the folk who hate you most.
Prowess and wealth are no defense
Against you, nor is sapience.
756 The noblest people, those with much
To live for, are the ones you clutch:

The youth, who counts on life and joy,
'Tis he whom you choose to destroy.
760 But when some beggar you descry,
Tottering, old, ready to die,
Suffering, praying for relief,
You turn a deaf ear to his grief.
764 To him who fears you you're adverse.
You're like a maundering child, or worse.
With fearful harm you penalize
Those whom you view with hostile eyes.
768 When you slew my friend, who was young
And craved for life, you did great wrong.
You sin once more, for I would die
And you pay no need to my cry.
772 You flee from me, Death. I pursue.
You hide from me. I'll seek for you.
When one's desire to die is strong,
You can't elude him very long.
776 When one who's suffering makes appeal
To you, you needs must turn your wheel.

HE THREATENS SUICIDE

'Pon my faith, I shall cease to pray
To you. Ere nightfall I shall slay
780 Myself. Life is a thing I hate
Now that I've lost my precious mate.
My soul shall follow close behind her
And in the flowery fields shall find her.
784 She'll come to meet me, gathering flowers.
She trusted the love that was ours:
I'll follow her without delay,
And die for her this very day.
788 This very day I'll join her where
She awaits me 'mid the blossoms fair."
Therewith he rose up to his feet
Like one intent his love to greet.

792   He drew his stylus forth. It gleamed
       With silver. Greatly he esteemed
       It, for 'twas given him by Blanchefleur
       The last time that he spoke to her
796   The day that he left for Montoire.
       Hear now the words spoken by Floire:
       "Stylus," he cried out, "you were meant
       For this, to finish my lament.
800   You are a token of her deep
       Love, something I should prize and keep.
       Stylus, do what you should and must.
       Send me to her. 'Tis only just.
804   Blanchefleur must take it much amiss
       That I have not died before this."

THE QUEEN STOPS HIM

       He made to plunge it in his heart
       When the queen saw him. With a start
808   She pounced on him, took from his hand
       The blade, with gentle reprimand.
       Mothers are mothers: such a blow
       Was more than she could undergo.
812   Said she: " 'Tis childish, my dear son,
       Thus to seek your extinction.
       Any person who could contrive
       To dodge death and to stay alive
816   Would rather be a leper, dwell
       Despised in wretched cot or cell,
       Than fall beneath Death's fatal stroke.
       To suffer death, son, is no joke.
820   If now you die by your own hand
       You'll go to no sweet-flowering land
       Nor see Blanchefleur. You must beware:
       Sinners are not admitted there.
824   Hell will assert claims none can flout,
       And there you'll go, son, beyond doubt.
       Minos, Thoas, Radamadus

There sit in judgment rigorous.
828   In hell these magistrates hold court.
They'll give you tortures of the sort
Borne by Dido and Bilitis
Who died when their love went amiss,
832   And weeping explore hell's domain
Seeking their lovers, all in vain:
Each one seeks and will seek the lover
Whom she can never more recover.
836   My fair dear son, be comforted.
You'll have her sooner live than dead,
I think there's potion to restore
The girl, and make her live once more."

She Moves the King to Mercy

840   Weeping, she sought the king straightway.
"Sire," said she, "listen to me, pray.
I beg you, by God the most great,
To your child be compassionate.
844   Stylus in hand he would have slain
Himself. I was there to restrain
Him, and, perceiving his intent
I took away his instrument."
848   "Dame," said he, "do not press me so.
He will recover from this blow."
"Indeed he will," she made reply,
"The way he'll do so is to die.
852   We have no children save this boy,
Whom by our own choice we destroy.
Throughout the land, men with one voice
Will say we killed him by our choice."
856   "What shall we do, madame, think you?"
"Let's tell him, fair lord?" "Ah yes, do."
The mother, hastening to obey,
Sought out her child without delay.

Floire Learns the Truth

860 "Dear son," said she, "this was a ruse
Of which your sire and I made use.
She's not dead. This tomb was designed
And built because we had in mind
864 That you'd forget her and would wed
Some girl of nobler rank instead,
Perhaps some King's fair daughter who
Would bring honor to us and you.
868 We both would very much prefer
That you, son, should not love Blanchefleur,
A girl of Christian parentage,
A poor thing of base lineage.
872 Merchants have purchased her, and they
Have borne her to lands far away.
'Tis as I say, son," said the dame,
"Therefore I beg you in God's name
876 Give up this sorrowing and cease
To grieve. Dwell here with us in peace."
"Is this the true tale?" asked the youth.
"Son, you may soon see it is truth."
880 They cause the stone to be removed.
Finding no trace of her he loved,
He praised God in heartfelt thanksgiving
To learn his true love was still living,
884 And said he too would live until
He found her if it were God's will.

He Declares He Will Find Blanchefleur

To seeking her he will devote
Himself: no land is so remote
888 But that he'll find her there and bring
Her back blissful and triumphing.
He heeds not, — being so possessed
With joy — the hardships of the quest.

892 Be not amazed, sirs. Understand
That one who obeys Love's command
Is certain he can carry out
Tasks that would put all men to rout.
896 Calcides and Plato have said it:
There's scarcely any one who'd credit
That such tasks can be carried through
As those who're ruled by Love can do.
900 That she's alive gives him such cheer
And joy that, heedless who may hear,
He says that though the king demur
He'll have no other maid than her.
904 Straightway to see the king he went.
The king was happy and content,
But his contentment changed to woe
When his son asked his leave to go
908 And seek this maid, of whom no one
Could say for certain where she'd gone
And none knew where it would be best
For him to undertake his quest.
912 He blames the queen for having told
Him he should have the maiden sold,
Curses the hour when to his cost
He did so: now they both are lost.
916 He'd give her price back, and would add
A thousand marks, and still be glad
Could he find her, but 'twould avail
Nought. Though he try he needs must fail.

THE KING RELUCTANTLY CONSENTS

920 "Son, pray remain here," said the king.
"Father, why ask me such a thing?
To have us both back, it were best
For you to speed me on my quest."
924 The father, weeping bitterly
To see his son go, made reply:
"Since your mind's made up, let me know

In what direction you would go,
928   Since go you must. I shall accede
To your wish, find you what you need:
Rich fabrics, gold and silver too,
Fine horses, splendid retinue."

EQUIPMENT FOR THE SEARCH

932   "Sire," said the young man, "hear, I pray,
Graciously what I have to say:
Dressed as a merchant I shall make
My search. Pack-horses seven I'll take.
936   Two shall bear silver, gold, and plate
Which I shall choose and stipulate.
The third upon his back shall bear
Coined dinars, enough and to spare.
940   The next two, cloth of every kind,
The very finest you can find.
Then two laden with furs, of sable
And marten, pelts invaluable.
944   This troop of seven beasts requires
Seven grooms, and I shall need three squires
Who'll carry food to serve our needs
As well as take care of our steeds.
948   Your chamberlain too. I request
That he accompany my quest,
For he knows how to buy and sell,
And he knows much that he can tell
952   Me when I need. Forth we shall fare,
Seeking our quarry everywhere,
And these resources should suffice,
If we can find her, for the price
956   That's asked. Ungrudgingly we'll pay
And then return without delay."
Thus the prince. His father concurred
And honorably kept his word,
960   Duly providing everything.
When time to take leave came, the king

Gave orders that the cup he'd got
For Blanchefleur's purchase should be brought.
964 "Son," said he, "place this in your pack:
Through it perhaps you'll get her back.
We've had it since the day when we
Sold your love, Blanchefleur, oversea."

A WONDERFUL HORSE

968 The king gave him a palfrey. It
Was his own, well-equipped and fit.
This horse on one side was pure white,
Blood-red on the side opposite.
972 But one spot of vermilion
Could be seen on his head upon
The white side, while the croup was pied
With one white spot on the red side.
976 The saddle-cloth, of fabric fine,
Was wrought in a chess-board design.
The saddle, and the pommel on
It, were made of a fish's bone:
980 Unstained and natural, its hue
Of a bewildering red and blue.
'Twas carved in fashion capital;
Set with skill was the martingale.
984 The saddle-cover of this horse
Was brown silk of Castillian source
Flowered with gold embroidering
To suit the pleasure of the king.
988 Cruppers, stirrup-thongs, cinches, all
Were of fine silk material
And all most wonderfully laced,
With buckles made of silver chased.
992 The stirrup-bars, of niello wrought
And gold, a castle would have bought.
No knight's harness ever displayed
Bridle more beautifully made.
996 The head-piece, made of fine gold, shone

With many a priceless precious stone;
In white enamel, here and there,
Were set these sparkling jewels rare.
1000   I can not — nor would it be meet —
Describe them in detail complete.
The bridle was of gold from Spain
And of workmanship sovereign.
1004   There are great virtues in each gem,
Precious and rare, each one of them.
The reins were pure gold. Never were
There reins richer nor handsomer.
1008   These gifts that the king gave him won
The gratitude of his young son.

A WONDERFUL RING

The queen for her part placed her ring
On his finger, admonishing
1012   Him: "My son, guard this with discretion.
Fear nought while it's in your possession.
Iron can not injure you nor maim,
Nor can fire burn you with its flame.
1016   You may trust its effectiveness,
Such power doth the ring possess.
While you wear it you are secure
Against failure or discomfiture."
1020   He took the ring, thanked her, and then
Said he'd find his sweetheart again.
He asked the king's leave to depart
Which the king gave with heavy heart.
1024   Of his mother he made like request;
She gave it, with seven kisses blessed
Him. They both shed tears of despair
And beat their breasts and tore their hair.
1028   You would have thought, to hear their cries,
He was dying before their eyes.
They thought they'd never see the youth
Again. Nor did they so in truth.

1032 The young prince, ready to depart,
   Tearful and with an anguished heart,
   Said "Vale." They in deep dejection,
   Commended him to God's protection.

Floire sets forth

1036 Behold him now as he proceeds
   Forth with his sumpter-beasts and steeds,
   And with the steward counseling
   About their plans for travelling.
1040 Their first goal, so they thought, should be
   The port whence Blanchefleur went to sea.
   Reaching this port at last, they then
   Took lodging with a citizen.
1044 Their beasts having been led away
   To the stables, with good oats and hay,
   The grooms in charge of them went down
   To the meat-merchants in the town.
1048 They found a butcher there who could
   Provide ample supply of food,
   And with the meat, and bread and wine,
   Arranged a supper rich and fine.
1052 As travelling merchants they proclaim
   Themselves, to cross the sea their aim.
   Floire is their lord, they make it known:
   The merchandise his, not their own.
1056 When their arrangements are complete,
   Before they seat themselves to eat,
   They wash, they lay the cloths, and make
   Things neat, then of their food partake.
1060 Their host was staunch and dignified;
   The young prince sat down by his side,
   Treating him with well-mannered care
   And urging him to share their fare.
1064 Ample supply of food was placed
   Before them, all cooked to their taste.
   The servants served it well, and poured

Wine for all seated at the board,
1068   With spiced and honeyed wine filled up
Silver hanap and golden cup.
The merchants, weary men and spent,
Ate and drank to their hearts' content.
1072   The good wine made it seem to some
That to Saint Martin's inn they'd come: *
They revel joyously and drink.
Only of Blanchefleur can Floire think
1076   Not for good wine is she forgot.
Without her, life to him means nought.
He seemed confused and stupefied
At times, and dolefully he sighed.
1080   Reaching for food, he did not look
Nor care if bread or meat he took.

An observant hostess

The hostess watched him at the board
And with her elbow nudged her lord.
1084   "Sir," said she, "have you chanced to see
This young man's eccentricity?
He's rapt in thought. He puts aside
His food. And ofttimes he has sighed.
1088   He is no merchant, that I'll swear,
But noble, and his mind's elsewhere."
She broached the subject to the youth:
"You are lost in thought, sir, that's the truth.
1092   I've watched you. You are neither drinking
Nor eating. You're absorbed in thinking.
'Twould cost but trifling sum to pay
For all you've eaten here today.

News of Blanchefleur

1096   The other day I saw the same
Behavior in a girl. Her name

---

* The name of this saint was commonly attached to good cheer and hospitality. See Pelan's note, p. 156.

Was Blanchefleur. She resembled you
So much. Upon my faith it's true.
1100 She might be the same age. You are
In face and features similar.
She too ate not, but, lost in dreams,
Was mourning for her friend, it seems.
1104 His name was Floire, she said, and they
Had sold her to get her away
From him. That is why she spoke not.
'Twas here, at this port, she was bought,
1108 Those who had purchased her declared
That 'twas to Babylon they fared
With her: the emir would pay twice
What they'd spent for her purchase-price."
1112 When these clear words had made it plain
That 'twas she, he could not restrain
His joy. Struck wordless, the young lover
Was so upset that he knocked over
1116 The cup before him which was filled
With wine, and all the wine was spilled.
The host cried out: "It's up to you
To pay the forfeit that is due."
1120 "Right so!" they all vociferated,
Gay, cheerful, and exhilarated.
Floire ordered that a cup of fine
Gold should be filled with good sound wine,
1124 And, offering the cup to her,
Said: "Dame, this gift I now confer
On you. 'Tis yours. Empty or fill
It as you please. Do what you will.
1128 This is the way that you are paid
For tidings of Blanchefleur the maid.
She is that maid for loss of whom I
Have been preoccupied and gloomy.
1132 I seek her, and I did not know
In which direction I should go."
She took the present that he made,
And thanked him, and to God she prayed
1136 That he might find the sweetheart whom

He sought, and gaily bring her home;
While he declared he would press on,
Barring hindrance, to Babylon.
1140 He added: "Wine that's gone to waste
Ought certainly to be replaced.
Therefore let all drink all the wine
They wish: let the expense be mine."
1144 Into the room came servants four:
Four sétiers of wine they bore,
From which they generously filled up
Silver hanap and golden cup.
1148 Floire was the first to drink a draught:
He passed it to the host, who quaffed,
Then all the others in the house,
Who joined with zest in the carouse.
1152 And anyone who was disposed
To get drunk did so unopposed;
The poorest man felt affluent
And boasted to his heart's content.
1156 They revelled, spirited and cheered,
And while they did so the wind veered.
The light was failing, night drew nigh
And in the port the flood rose high.
1160 The ship-captains declared the gale
Was over-strong for mast and sail.
Though eager to be on their way,
They had to endure long delay.

THEY TAKE SHIP FOR BABYLON

1164 Then, when at last the wind had died
Down, and the sea was pacified,
The seamen had cried forth the word
Through town that those should come aboard
1168 Who wished passage to Babylon
Or to the regions farther on.
With joy Floire heard the criers' shout
And he made ready to set out.

1172   He paid his followers and paid
The host at whose house he had stayed,
Took leave of him, as it was fit,
Went to the ship and boarded it.
1176   The skipper who was in command
Asked if he might set him on land
Where'er he could with greatest speed
Cast anchor. To this he agreed.
1180   He answered this sea-faring man:
"I wish to profit if I can
In Babylon the great stronghold,
For I have been advised and told
1184   That one month from this day will bring
To the emir's court a gathering
Of kings who owe to the emir
Their lands and who, from far and near,
1188   Come to a fête he's wont to give.
If at that time I could arrive
I think that I could promptly sell
My merchandise and profit well."
1192   What with clear air and a fair breeze
The ship could navigate with ease.
They hoisted all their sails on high
And used other means too whereby
1196   To make speed. The wind drove them on.
Now Floire's sea-faring has begun.
Aboard with him such following
He's brought as would suffice a king.
1200   Eight full days o'er the waters wide
They sailed, and still no land they spied.

THEY DISEMBARK AT BAUDUC

The ninth day to Bauduc they came,
A city of great might and fame.
1204   High o'er the port, upon the crown
Of a great dark cliff, stands the town:
Thence on clear days one easily

Can look a hundred leagues to sea.
1208   The ship-master knew how to keep
A straight and true course o'er the deep.
This was the port toward which he bore
And here he set the prince ashore.
1212   One can in four days from this port —
Winter days that are the most short
Of all — reach Babylon, with steeds
And baggage, if nothing impedes.
1216   The ship-master asked to be paid
And no reluctance Floire displayed:
Gladly of silver marks a score
He paid, of gold marks twenty more.
1220   He thought that 'twas on Heaven's strand
He'd disembarked, for in this land
He hoped to find the girl whom he
Had followed over land and sea.
1224   They take the baggage that was stowed
In the ship, then promptly they reload
And make their way up to the town
1226a   That on the landing-place looks down.

THEY LODGE WITH A MERCHANT

They lodged there with a townsman, one
1228   Of wealth and reputation,
A merchant and a mariner
As well. Two of his great ships were
In port: with them he plied his trade
1232   And oversea his goods conveyed
When need be. 'Twas in one of these
That those merchants had crossed the seas
Who bought Blanchefleur whom Floire now sought
1236   And through whose loss he was distraught.
It was at this man's house therefore
They slept the night they came ashore,
For Floire thought he might be the one
1240   To tell them where the maid had gone.

The chamberlain had had the sacks
Removed from the pack-horses' backs,
Had the beasts bedded down and saw
1244   They were well-fed and had fresh straw.
Sirs, they found all they wished to buy,
And bought it, in this hostelry,
Hay, oats, excellent wines, and fresh
1248   Chickens, and fresh and salted flesh.
They did not linger in preparing
Their food, being worn out with sea-faring.
The port belonged to the emir
1252   And many men have troubles here:
Rightly or wrongly, those who land
Here are perforce obliged to hand
The provost all their property,
1256   Then swear to their veracity. *
When all this had been done, and when
The food had been prepared, the men
Washed their hands and sat down to eat,
1260   With Floire in the most honored seat
Their food was of the very best
And they devoured it with great zest.

THEIR HOST GIVES NEWS OF BLANCHEFLEUR

But Floire, with Blanchefleur on his mind,
1264   Was obviously disinclined
To eat. This fact the host perceived
And was somewhat distressed and grieved.
"You're worried, sir, it seems to me,"
1268   He said, "about your property:
Our customs trouble you, of course."
"Sir, my cares have a different source,"
Said Floire. "Just such inquietude,"
1272   The host said, "in this inn I viewed

---

* See Pelan's note on this passage, which is obscure. It seems to refer
to a customs office.

The other day. There was a band
Of merchants, merchants from the land
Of Spain, whence they had come direct.
1276   They had with them, I recollect
A maiden who behaved, I vow,
Much as you are behaving now.
Blanchefleur I heard her called. And on
1280   My vessel she was woebegone.
At mealtimes she too, all forlorn,
For her lost friend would brood and mourn."
Hearing this, Floire great joy displayed.
1284   Said he: "What happened to the maid?"
"To Babylon they took their course,"
The host said, "and she too perforce."

HE IS REWARDED

Floire gave the host a cloak of vair
1288   And a gold cup of beauty rare.
"Sir, 'tis my wish that you have these.
Tender your thanks to Blanchefleur, please.
It is in search of her I've come;
1292   She was stolen from me, from my home."
The host thanked him: "May God restore
Your lady love to you once more!"
When they had eaten all that they
1296   Could, servants cleared the cloths away.
Beds were set up. Weary and spent,
The men lay down at once and went
To sleep. And while Floire slept and dreamed,
1300   He spoke with Blanchefleur, so it seemed
To him, Blanchefleur his well-loved treasure,
And this gave him no end of pleasure.
He slept, but he did not sleep on
1304   Too long; at the first light of dawn
At once he woke his retinue.

Onward to Babylon by Road

When things had all been packed anew
They took the road which should lead straight
1308   Onward to Babylon the great.
They stopped the evening of that day
At a fine caravanserai,
And the next morning, at the break
1312   Of early dawn, fresh start they make.
And at the day's end settle down
In quarters in a market-town.
There they had word of her anew,
1316   For folk had seen her passing through.
The third day ere sundown they came
To an inlet of the sea. Its name
Was Frelle, the local people say.
1320   Across the stream Montfelix lay.
The master of this rich chateau
Ferried travellers to and fro.
There was no plank nor bridge. Too deep
1324   The gully was, and very steep.
But close beside the bank, and borne
Upon a stake, there hung a horn.
To call the boatman, one would blow
1328   The horn for passage to or fro.
One of the party blew a blast
Which brought the ferryman in haste.
The master promptly took aboard
1332   In his own boat the youthful lord.
The servants with the boatman rode.
The sumpter-beasts, each with its load
Of goods, crossed in the barge. They then
1336   Set forth, merchants and ferrymen.

A Ferryman Gives More News

The master scanned the young lord's face
And, judging him of noble race,

1340 Asked: "Whither are you bound?" and he
Replied to him: "Do you not see?
I am a merchant man, and I
Am going to Babylon to buy
Goods, and to sell these wares of mine
1344 Which, as you see, are very fine.
If your château has room to spare,
Grant us tonight, pray, lodging there."
"I've room, sir," said he, "you are right,
1348 And I will shelter you tonight.
But, sir, the reason for my query,
Was that you looked dismal and dreary,
And one who looked exactly so
1352 I saw, not half a year ago:
It was a young girl and she passed
Through here, similarly downcast.
You look like her, my faith, 'tis true.
1356 I know not if she's kin to you."
When he heard this, Floire raised his head.
"And where did this girl go?" he said.
"She went to Babylon from here,
1360 Where she was bought by the emir."

FLOIRE ASKS FOR AID

Floire said nothing at all, but kept
His counsel. In the château they slept
That night. At dawn, having reposed,
1364 He rose and took leave of his host.
But before that a gift he made him
Of a hundred sous. Likewise he prayed him
That if in Babylon some friend
1368 He knew who'd help him gain his end,
He'd send some sign this friend would heed
And give counsel in time of need.
"Before you come to Babylon,
1372 My lord," he said, "you'll come upon
A water very wide and deep,

And him whose task it is to keep
The bridge you will encounter there.
1376   He is my friend and my confrère.
In Babylon he holds high station:
House, tower, wealth, fine situation.
He's my associate in these
1380   Two crossings, and we share the fees.
Take him this ring of mine, and make
It known to him that for my sake
He is to counsel you as best
1384   He can. I'm sure lodging and rest
He'll give you." Thus adieu they say.
They reached the bridge before mid-day,
And there they crossed. At the bridge-head
1388   A poplar-tree its branches spread;
Beneath this tree the tollman, seated
Upon a block of marble, greeted
Them. Well-dressed, fair, he gave the impression
1392   Of one of merit and discretion.
Four deniers payment was required
Of every person who desired
To cross, and for his horse like fee.
1396   Floire greeted with due courtesy
This vassal; and then having spoken
In all the gods' names, gave him the token,
His partner's ring, with the request
1400   For hospitality and rest,
For friendly comradeship and wise
Suggestion, should the need arise.

A FRIENDLY TOLLMAN

This man, as soon as he espied
1404   The ring, gladly identified
It, took it and gave him his own;
Then to his wife he sent him on,
Who'd give them welcome. Next he showed
1408   Then the château where he abode.

Thither they went, and there the ring
Won them a cordial welcoming,
A lodging bright and comfortable
1412   As well as ample barn and stable.
Floire has arrived at last where he
Had ardently desired to be,
Well-lodged, with the toll-man for host.
1416   Advice is what he needs the most.
Though he has managed now to find
The goal on which he'd set his mind,
He is unsure, and in great need
1420   Of counsel on how to proceed.

FLOIRE'S INNER STRUGGLE

Wisdom arrives to take her place
In his heart, to recall his race
And rank, tell him he is unwise.
1424   "Floire," she inquires, "who can advise
You? You know no one, not a soul,
With whom you can discuss your goal.
You'd be a fool if you confessed
1428   It, seriously or in jest.
For should your folly reach his ear,
There's little doubt that the emir
Would order your immediate
1432   Arrest. Hanging would be your fate.
Be wise: go back home. Change your mind.
Your father will be glad to find
A wife for you, a girl of high
1436   Exalted rank and ancestry."
Said Love: "What nonsense! Fie, for shame!
Go home without the girl you came
To rescue? Home without the sole
1440   Aim of your journey, your sole goal?
Have you forgotten how you drew
Your blade the other day, when you
Were bound to kill yourself for love?

1444 And now it's home you're thinking of!
If you were there and she were here,
You'd come straight back here, never fear.
And you could live without her, think

1448 You? You have had too much to drink!
Without her, even though you had
The world's gold, you could not be glad
Or happy. Stay here. You will see

1452 Her, take her home with you, maybe.
It's hard to keep chained down or tied
The beast that longs to be outside.
If she perceives you, she will seek

1456 And find some ruse, some means, to speak
To you. Lovers, I know possess
Surpassing guile and artfulness.
The peasant says: 'He whose works please

1460 God, labors swiftly and with ease.' "
And thus within his heart Love fought
This fight, and he was much distraught.
The host came in. Seeing him thus

1464 Down-hearted and lugubrious,
He spoke to him straightforwardly.
"Fair sir, most noble youth," said he,
"Is something preying on your mind?

1468 Are you ill-lodged here? If you find
Something that is not to your taste
I'll have it remedied in haste."
"Sir," he replied, "with kindly thought

1472 And grace you speak, but there is nought
In this your hostel that's not fit
And fine. I pray God to permit
Me, good sir, fitly to reward

1476 Your welcome and your friendly word.
What makes me worried and upset
Is the merchandise I've come to get.
I fear lest I may not espy it,

1480 Or, if I do, that I can't buy it."

A SPLENDID FEAST

The host, a good man and discreet,
Replied: "My lord, let us now eat.
Then, if my art and skill suffice,
1484 I'll gladly give you my advice."
To dinner without more ado
They went. The host called his wife too.
The prince was placed between the pair,
1488 Dame Licoris and the host, Daire,
A feast rich and elaborate
Was served in gold and silver plate.
There was great quantity of fine
1492 Clear wine, and spiced and honeyed wine.
For meat there was profusion
Of varied cuts of venison,
Cranes, partridges, herons; with these
1496 Swans too, and peacocks, and wild geese,
In such abundance, one and all
Could feast on them, both great and small.
The host, Daire, then had servants bring
1500 In fruit, for further pleasuring:
Pomegranates, figs, pears, to please
The taste, sorbs, almonds, quantities
Of luscious fruits of every kind
1504 The best fruits anyone could find.
Peaches there were, and chestnuts, for
The city had fruits in great store.
On these fruits happily they dine,
1508 Ending their meal with draughts of wine.
Floire viewed the cup of rich device
That had been Blanchefleur's purchase-price.
It stood before him, filled with wine
1512 Pellucid, clear, and crystalline.
Upon it Helen's image shone,
Hand held by Paris, her loved one.
As he upon this image gazed,
1516 Love kindled warm his heart and raised

His spirit, saying: "Have good cheer.
See! Paris leads his sweetheart here."
"Ah God! And shall I see the day
1520 When I thus lead Blanchefleur away?"
"Come, Floire! As soon as dinner's through
Your host is going to counsel you."
The long dinner made him morose.
1524 The dame eyed him meanwhile with close
Attention. She knew he was torn
By inward strife, sad and forlorn.
She saw the flowing tears that trace
1528 Their way down his young tender face,
And pityingly called her lord's
Attention to them, though no words
She spoke. The cloths are cleared away.
1532 Only those three at table stay.

FLOIRE IDENTIFIES HIMSELF

"My dear young lord," observed the host,
"If you're disturbed and discomposed,
Tell me just why you're so distressed,
1536 And I shall counsel you as best
I can. Do not keep hidden your
True state. 'Tis make-believe, I'm sure,
That selling cloth is what you've planned.
1540 You've other business in hand."
"Upon my faith," said Licoris,
"Looking at him, it seems to me
That he is beautiful Blanchefleur.
1544 I'm certain he is twin to her.
This young lord has the self-same grace,
Like mien, like figure, and like face:
Face and demeanor both convince
1548 Me she's close kin to this young prince.
She was here but two weeks ago;
Sore was her heartache, sore her woe
For Floire her sweetheart. Day and night

1552   She wept, bewailing her sad plight.
        And when, purchased by the emir,
        She had to go away from here,
        I saw how the poor damsel grieved."

1556   Floire with bewilderment received
        This. "Dame, I was lost in thought," said he.
        I'm her brother, my sister she."
        "Have no fear, friend," said Daire. "It's true

1560   You know what kin she is to you.
        But you misstate the truth a bit:
        It's foolish thus to alter it.
        " 'Tis so," the young man made reply,

1564   "I'm a king's son, I'll certify.
        Blanchefleur is my sweet friend, 'fore God,
        Stolen away from me by fraud.

He Reveals His Mission

        I've come to this country, pursuing
1568   Her, unsure what I'd best be doing.
        I've gold and silver: well-to-do
        Am I. I'll shower wealth on you,
        If you'll advise me, help me find

1572   A means. For I've made up my mind.
        One of two things: I shall recover
        Her, or die because I love her."
        "Prince, 'twere a shame most melancholy

1576   Were you to perish for such folly.
        I should not dare boast that I could
        Really advise you for your good.
        The best counsel I have you'll hear

1580   Now, if you're bound to persevere.

Discouraging Counsel

        You can't succeed. And I dare say
        Your life will be the price you pay.

Should the emir hear this report, your
1584 Doom will be a death with torture.
In this land even the mightiest man
Who'd dare to undertake such plan
For all his wealth and mightiness
1588 Could not, I know, achieve success.
Not magic nor chicanery
Would e'er avail to set her free.
If all the men who are alive
1592 On earth, or who have lived, should strive
By force to take her, they would meet
At the emir's hands sure defeat.
Seven score kings and ten obey
1596 His jurisdiction, own his sway.
They're called to Babylon? Excuse
Avails not: they can not refuse.

BABYLON DESCRIBED

Full twenty leagues does Babylon
1600 Extend in one direction.
No low wall guards the city. It
Is soundly built, with stones that fit
Firmly, with solid mortar, so
1604 That it fears not a steel pike's blow;
Being full three fathoms high, 'tis made
To face onslaught or escalade.
Four score gates are set in the wall,
1608 All wide, stout and substantial.
On each of the week's eight days, there
Is held inside the walls a fair.
In Babylon rise towers galore,
1612 Seven hundred of them and more.
In these the enfoeffed barons dwell.
They fortify the citadel:
The least and flimsiest could defy
1616 The Roman emperor's soldiery
For fifteen years, and hold at bay

His force. Spacious and strong are they.
Babylon can not be subdued
1620 By one man or by multitude
Of men. Neither is it alarmed
By treason, so well is it armed.
A tower of great antiquity
1624 In mid-city soars loftily,
Made all of marble blocks cut square,
Vaulted, no columns anywhere.
The tower has battlements: its spire
1628 Rises a full fifty feet higher,
Covered with Apulia's gold,
The finest, splendid to behold,
And, to adorn its topmost height,
1632 A hundred marks of silver bright.
Upon the pinnacle was placed
A carbuncle that fiercely blazed.
'Twas set there with great skill. It shone
1636 At night as if it were the sun,
And no lad was obliged to bear
The slightest torch or candle there.
Knights, merchants, others, thither bound
1640 Never have need to look around
After night-fall: it's safe to say
That such folk can not go astray,
Whether land-faring or sea-faring:
1644 They're not obliged to take a bearing.
Though twenty leagues off, its bright beam
Only a league away will seem.

THE TOWER OF MAIDENS

This tower has three levels. He
1648 Who made them had great artistry.
The columns are of marble all,
Free of sustaining prop or wall,
Yet one pillar is adequate
1652 To hold with ease the whole tower's weight,

Surging from the deepest foundation
To the steeple's topmost elevation.
It's made of marble white, inlaid
1656   With crystal, and inside is made
A channel through which mounts a spring
Of waters cool, clear, strengthening.
These waters to the third floor rise;
1660   I think the engineer was wise
Who had the skill to make this fount
Along the pillar's flank thus mount
To the upper floors, and find its place in
1664   A neatly painted metal basin.
The girls who are quartered there proceed
To wash their hands in it as need
Requires. The tower doth enclose
1668   Rooms seven score. The water flows
To each. Who dwells there suffers not.
The pillars are of crystal wrought;
The roof is made of plane-tree wood
1672   Which lasts forever, sound and good.
Fashioned of ebony and clear
Glass* were the windows. The emir
Had caused great labor to be spent
1676   Upon the tower's embellishment
And structure; no reptile can make
Entry there, adder, worm nor snake.
Whoever at the paintings looks
1680   With care learns much that's writ in books,
For ancient stories there are told,
Wars, prowess, noble deeds of old.

The dwellers in the Tower

Within each room a maiden dwells:
1684   The emir's lovely damosels

---

* The O. F. word, *mirra,* is of uncertain meaning. Glass is a conjecture
of Godefroy.

They are, who when he's pleased to call,
Give service deferential.
From floor to floor they are conducted
1688   By stairways artfully constructed.
At mid-tower there is a door
Such as was never seen before
Or since, and through this door one comes
1692   Down to the emir's private rooms.
Through this portal they come and go,
These maids whom he summons below
And whose duty is to obey
1696   And serve his will in every way.
Seven score maids, of noble race
And lovely, therein spend their days.
The Tower of Maidens, people call
1700   It, since they're maidens one and all.
Two groups of those who dwell there carry
On some small service customary.
By order of the emir they
1704   Must wait on him at his levée.
With fear to this task they addressed
Themselves, though each girl did her best.

THE GUARDIANS OF THE TOWER

The watchmen in the tower have all
1708   Been shorn of organs genital.
Stationed on each floor there are three,
With one chief whose authority
Over the other nine extends.
1712   Each of the nine humbly attends
The girls, makes beds, and serves their food.
Their chief is evil, fierce, and rude:
He mounts guard on the outer gate,
1716   And there he serves, early and late,
With each hand clutching a fell arm,
1717a   A poniard and a gisarme.
In a dark corner stealthily

He lurks, a guardian shrewd and sly.
1720   If he sees someone loitering
Around and reconnoitering
The tower, he will, with expedition
And with the emir's full permission,
1724   In any way he likes mistreat him,
Plunder him, steal his goods, and beat him.
And, be it night or day, four sentries
Within the tower guard all the entries.
1728   If someone draws nigh, they're not slow
To warn the sentinels below.

THE CHOICE OF A WIFE, AND HER FATE

It is the way of the emir
To keep a wife one single year,
1732   One year and no more. Then he brings
Together all his dukes and kings.
She's then beheaded. His strict ban
Forbids cleric or nobleman
1736   To possess her whom his embrace
Has honored. He takes in her place
Another, whom he singles out
After the girls have all been brought
1740   Down to the garden where he makes
His choice. Each girl in terror quakes:
It is an honor that inspires
Dismay, since none of them desires
1744   To lose her life. Now you must hear
Of the garden, and why the emir
Calls them there. It is fair and spacious;
In all the world there's none more gracious.

THE GARDEN AND THE RIVER

1748   All about, forming an enclosure,
Is a wall painted gold and azure.

Each turret of the battlement
Is topped by a bird — each different
1752 From all the others — wrought and cast
In brass. And each in the wind's blast
Gives forth its individual sound
And cry. The wild beasts all around,
1756 Tigers, lions, and leopards, all
Grow tame and mild, hearing this call.
In fine weather this garden rings
With such varied and sweet warblings
1760 Of birds — some real, some fabricated —
Thrush, mavis, jay, in variegated
Tuneful and gay exuberance,
Cheering the garden's wide expanse,
1764 That he who hears the festive rhythm
Must grieve unless his sweetheart's with him.
Outside the garden, I surmise,
There flows a stream of Paradise:
1768 Euphrates is its name, and it
So hems it as not to permit
Entry to anything whatever, —
Unless it flies above the river.
1772 Precious stones lie within the stream:
No man ever saw gems with gleam
So bright: sapphire, chalcedony,
Jacinth, sardonyx gorgeously
1776 Aglow, jasper and crystal rare,
Enamels too that flash and flare,
And others I can not recall
Or name. I can not tell you all.
1780 The garden blooms, heedless of time
And season; bird-songs ring and chime;
There's no tree, be it rare or dear,
That can not be found growing here:
1784 Fig-tree, laurel, and service-tree,
With almond-tree and olive-tree.

And all the others that produce
Fruit grow and flourish here profuse.
1788 Pepper and cinnamon these groves
Give, frankincense, rosemary, cloves,
And other spices redolent,
Filling the air with sweetest scent:
1792 In no country, from east to west,
Is there aught like it, I'll attest.
A man who falls beneath the spell
Of this enchanting spicy smell
1796 And hears the birds singing away
The dulcet music of love's lay,
Might well believe that in some wise
He's been brought in to Paradise.
1800 Mid-garden flows a limpid spring,
Fresh, wholesome, and unfaltering;
Through a duct of silver pure, agleam
Like sparkling crystal, flows the stream.
1804 Above it grows a splendid tree:
Indeed, no man did ever see
Its like. The Tree of Love, men call
It. 'Tis in bloom perpetual:
1808 As each flower falls, one comes to fill
Its place. The tree was placed with skill.
Vermilion are both tree and flowers.
He was endowed with magic powers
1812 Who planted it. For such sagacity
Guided the placing of the tree,
The orient-rising morning sun
Pours its vermilion rays upon
1816 It, while two winds that blow and meet
There serve to moderate the heat.
It was arranged by art supernal
To make the blossoming eternal.

THE RITUAL OF CHOICE

1820 When the time comes for the emir
To choose, he summons his girls here

To the fresh spring waters which travel
Rippling o'er emeralds and gravel.
1824   When the maids come to cross the flume
Which crystal and silver illume,
They make the crossing one by one,
While he pays close attention
1828   To them, and so too do his kings.
Now you shall hear astounding things:
When a virgin crosses, the rill
Remains transparent, pure and still.
1832   While one whom man has known will spoil
Its calm, will muddy it and roil.
Such a one's end is grim and dire.
She's slain and cast into a fire.
1836   He makes them all walk — to decide
Which one this year will be his bride —
Beneath the tree. And she upon
Whom falls a blossom is the one.
1840   On destiny the choice depends:
She on whom the first bloom descends
Is crowned forthwith, and all acclaim
Her as the country's ruling dame.
1844   He weds her, treats her with high honor,
Lavishes loving care upon her
Until the year's end ends her reign
And he has her blinded or slain.

BLANCHEFLEUR IS THE OBVIOUS CHOICE

1848   If by chance there is one girl there
Whom he loves most or who's most fair,
He makes the flower, by necromancy,
Fall first on her who charms his fancy.
1852   A month from now will be the date
When the great lords will congregate
Who in his service are enrolled,
And on that day a feast he'll hold.
1856   Men say he'll pick Blanchefleur: beyond

All other damsels he is fond
Of her. Her beauty knows no peer.
That's why he'll wed her, 'twould appear.
1860   The services she renders fire
His heart and quicken his desire.
He's eager. He can hardly wait
For the present year to terminate."
1864   Said Floire: "Thank you, sir. If this be
The truth, 'twill be the death of me.
All that I live for will have died
If she becomes the emir's bride.
1868   Now, my good host, Daire, how prevent him?
I'll do my best to circumvent him.
What care I if I lose my life?
If he takes my sweetheart for wife
1872   I know he'll deal me a death blow.
But when she, Blanchefleur, comes to know
This, she who loves me tenderly,
She'll spurn his love completely: she
1876   Will strive to compass her own end,
Thus he will not have my sweet friend."

How to Bribe a Watchman

Daire answered: "Since I realize
That your heart's tangled in such wise
1880   That you show not the least concern
For life if she for whom you yearn
Is lost, hear me now! I'll suggest
A plan that seems to me the best.
1884   You'll go tomorrow and inspect
The tower. Act like an architect:
Measure its width and note with care
How high it rises in the air.
1888   The porter is a brutal bully.
He'll question you, and distrustfully.
Then you, to hoodwink him, will state
You mean to build its duplicate

1892   When you return home, and you came
        Here with that sole and single aim.
        From this he'll draw the inference
        That you're a man of affluence.

1896   He'll cultivate you and pursue
        Your friendship: He'll play chess with you.
        He loves to play chess, and he will
        With pleasure wager on his skill.

1900   Make sure to have your wallet hold
        A hundred ounces of good gold
        To wager on the game you play.
        Your life may be the price you pay

1904   If you do not. You must deceive
        And bribe the fellow, I believe.
        If you win, give him back his stake,
        And along with it let him take

1908   Your own. This gift will much amaze
        Him, win his gratitude and praise;
        And when you leave he'll make it plain
        He's like to play with you again.

1912   He'll urge you to come back next day
        And you'll consent to come and play
        Again. Twice as much cash you'll take.
        If you win, give him back his stake

1916   And yours as well. His gratitude
        And love for you will be renewed
        And even deeper than before:
        He'll pray you to return once more.

1920   You'll answer: "Gladly! For 'tis true
        I have grown very fond of you.
        I've ample gold and silver. I
        Shall be delighted to supply

1924   You with some, in appreciation
        Of your thoughtful consideration."
        Four hundred ounces the next day
        You'll bring. Your cup too you'll convey

1928   To the chessboard. If the victory fall
        To you, give him your gold and all
        His own, but hold tight to your cup.

He will suggest you put it up
1932 As stake for one more game. Be sure
You don't yield to this overture.
When he sees that you do not care
For further play, he'll bid you share
1936 His dinner. He'll be filled with glee
At all that gold of yours that he
Has won. He'll treat you at his table
With honor unexceptionable.
1940 He'll crave the cup: with greed he'll eye it,
And avidly will seek to buy it.
A thousand marks will be the price
That he will offer to entice
1944 You. Meet this with a firm rejection;
Then give it him for sheer affection.
He'll be so stunned and so cajoled
By this, so drunk with all your gold
1948 That he'll fall at your feet straightway
And offer gratefully to pay
You homage. This you will accept.

THE WATCHMAN WILL YIELD TO GREED

If he does not he'll be inept
1952 Indeed! I know that's what he'll do.
He will obey, whatever you
Command. And then you can disclose
What you think are your mortal woes.
1956 He'll do your pleasure and fulfill
In every way he can your will."
Hearing this, Floire hastened to thank
Daire for his counsel wise and frank.
1960 Before they go to bed they take
A last drink. Thought keeps Floire awake:
He rises at the break of day,
And then Daire speeds him on his way.

FLOIRE BEGINS HIS CAMPAIGN

1964   He reached the tower: he had all
The air of a man substantial
And sound. He took measures around
The base, and its height off the ground.

1968   The porter challenged him with crude
Words and with hostile attitude:
"You, fellow, who have got your eye
On our tower, I think you're a spy!"

1972   "Indeed I'm not, sir, that I swear.
I'm looking at it with great care.
When I return home, if I'm able,
I mean to build one comparable."

1976   This general air of affluence,
These words, spoken with confidence,
Impressed him. "You're no spy, I'd guess,"
He said, then asked him to play chess.

1980   Floire answered that he'd gladly play,
But for high stakes. "And how high, say?"
"A hundred marks of gold." "My coffer
Can match that. I accept your offer.

1984   And so they sat down for the test
Of skill. And Floire, who played the best,
Was winner of the contest. He
Gave the stake back immediately.

1988   This generosity amazed
The man, who gave him thanks and praised
Him, urging him to come and play
At chess with him another day.

THE CAMPAIGN PROCEEDS

1992   He did so, and as he'd been told
Brought two hundred ounces of gold
With him. The porter matched them and
Once more Floire got the upper hand,

1996   And once more gave back the whole sum.

The porter, who at first was dumb
With joy, when once he could recover
His speech swore to serve him forever,
2000 And when Floire left, with eagerness
Asked him to play again at chess.
The next day Floire returned once more.
This time the golden cup he bore,
2004 And with it he did not forget
Four hundred marks of gold to bet.
The porter brought from out his hoard
Like sum. Each placed upon the board
2008 His chessmen, and the porter took
Great care to set them. With his rook
Floire captured pieces numerous,
Then said "check," and the porter thus
2012 Became aware, to his chagrin,
That he had no more chance to win.
He paid his gold, in some distress,
But Floire revived his happiness
2016 By giving back all he had won,
The porter's wager and his own.
The fellow felt he had been bested,
But then politely he suggested
2020 The cup as stake when next they played
A match. "Ah, by no means!" Floire made
Reply. The man urged, pleaded, then
Asked Floire to dine with him again.
2024 The flow of gold that swelled his treasure
Roused his affection beyond measure.
The cup above all with avidity
He craves. It stirs all his cupidity.
2028 For a thousand marks of gold he tries
To buy it, truly a high price.
Floire, seeing the man's greed stirred up
And tense, in his hands placed the cup,
2032 Saying: "It is not my intent
To sell you this. I shall present
It to you. I'm sure you'll repay
Me if I need your help some day."

The porter swears allegiance

2036 He takes the cup, swears to fulfill
      Floire's wishes and obey his will.
      After the swearing of this oath
      The gatekeeper and young Floire both
2040 Desired to take their ease. They strolled
      Into the garden. There they hold
      Confab. The man offers to do
      Homage. Floire takes it, wisely too!
2044 "As my own man I now rely
      On you," says Floire, "Now list while I
      Explain my situation:
      My friend is in that tower yon.
2048 She is the one who's named Blanchefleur,
      I'm so distraught by love for her
      That I've come all the way from Spain
      To seek her out in this domain.
2052 Pity me, pray. You understand
      I've placed my whole life in your hand.
      And that, sir, is the tale in brief:
      I'll have her, or I'll die of grief."

He regrets his greed

2056 At this, the porter, disconcerted
      And upset, said: "I've been subverted
      By your wealth, basely put upon
      By cunning and deception.
2060 My own greed put me off my guard.
      Your love will make death my reward.
      But since it's thus, I can do nought,
      Nor turn back: in the snare I'm caught.
2064 So, whether good or ill ensue,
      I shall not fail my pledge to you,
      Though I am certain 'pon my faith
      All three of us are doomed to death.

2068   Return now to your hostelry
   And in three days come back to me:
   Meanwhile I shall devote my thought
   To hatching some insidious plot."
2072   Floire, tearful and disconsolate.
   Said: "That's a long, long time to wait."
   "Ah, no indeed! 'Tis very short:
   Death is my lot," was the retort,
2076   "My good sir Floire, you do not care
   A great deal just how this affair
   May finish. So you see your friend,
   You're willing for your life to end."

A FLOWERY STRATAGEM

2080   Floire left the garden. Now the man
   Conceived a cunning guileful plan:
   He prepared baskets, filled and laden
   With blossoms, as seeming gifts to gladden
2084   The hearts of the young girls who lived
   In the tower. The third day arrived;
   Prince Floire returned, a joyous lover,
   His hours of waiting being over.
2088   He had been well advised to don
   A tunic of vermilion.
   The porter then, as I have said,
   Heaped baskets full of roses red.
2092   He sent to each and every maiden
   A basket thus fragrantly laden,
   Floire enters one, over his head
   A covering of roses spread,
2096   By blossoms sweet concealed from sight.
   Meanwhile he keeps is eyes closed tight.
   The porter calls two servants. "Stay
   Not," said he. "This you will convey
2100   Into yon tower, to the high cell
   Wherein Lady Blanchefleur doth dwell.
   It's on the landing where the stair

Leads to the emir's bed; and there
2104 You'll leave it. Tell her that I sent
It. I am sure the compliment
Will please her. She will hold it dear.
When you have done this, come back here."
2108 They lift the basket, find the weight
Excessive and immoderate:
"These flowers are like to break one's back,"
They say, cursing the man who'd pack
2112 Them thus. So up the tower they clamber.

THE WRONG ROOM

But then they enter the wrong chamber.
Blanchefleur's is on the right. Misled,
They take the left-hand door instead.
2116 Entering this room, they hand over
The flowers to her whom they discover
Therein. Their message they impart
To her in haste, in haste depart.
2120 She thanks them for the gift they bring,
She strokes the flowers, their fragrance drinks.
This is his loved one, so Floire thinks,
2124 And out he leaps, filled with delight.
The girl in wonder and affright
Can not restrain her shocked surprise
At this strange sight. "Ai! Ai!" she cries.
2128 Back to his hiding-place Floire scurried.
Small wonder if he's scared and worried.
He has lost his friend, he thinks. He's made
A blunder; he has been betrayed.
2132 So dexterously does Floire hide
That nothing of him shows outside.
All the girls, when they hear the shout,
Hasten to her room, crowd about
2136 Her, asking what has given rise
To her disturbance and her cries.

Her fears stilled, it occurs to her
That this has to do with Blanchefleur.
2140   This is the sweetheart, she believes,
For whom Blanchefleur so often grieves.

A RESOURCEFUL GIRL

Therefore, with great presence of mind,
A ruse she manages to find:
2144   "A butterfly flew from within
These flowers. Its wings struck my chin,
And being somewhat terrified,
I gave a sudden start, and cried."
2148   Laughing, the other girls regained
Their rooms. She with the prince remained:
A German duke's young daughter, she
Was Blanchefleur's favorite company.
2152   Holding each other very dear,
Together they served the emir.
Fairer was she than anyone
In the tower, save Blanchefleur alone.
2156   Blanchefleur's basket came. With small spirit
She viewed it, scarcely even went near it.
Her room is just across the hall
And she speaks little if at all.
2160   Her joyless reveries scarcely stray
From her beloved, night or day.
The two girls' chambers were located
Side by side. They communicated
2164   Through a door when either was inclined
To tell what she had on her mind.
Claris was the girl's name. And she
Spoke now to Blanchefleur tenderly:
2168   "Blanchefleur, my sweet companion,
Won't you look at a fair flower, one
Which I am certain you will treasure
And love and cherish beyond measure,
2172   Once you have seen it? Well I know

In this land no such flower doth grow.
Look at it. If you recognize
It, you shall have it for your prize."
2176 Said Blanchefleur: "Claris, friend most dear,
Why do you mock at me and jeer?
My faith! 'Tis unkind. You transgress
When you make sport of my distress.
2180 The girl who savors love's content
It is for her that flowers are meant.
Sweet sister Claris, I am sure
This my life will not long endure:
1284 The emir means to have me, goes
The gossip. It's true, I suppose
But, so it please God, he shall not.
Nor shall reproach ever be brought
2188 Against me, nor men say that ever
Blanchefleur left Floire for any lover.
For love of Floire I'll find a way
To kill myself without delay.
2192 Sweet sister, should I so offend
My Floire, I should have no more friend."

THE LOVERS ARE REUNITED

The girl listened with deep compassion,
Then, tenderly, spoke in this fashion:
2196 "For love of him I now entreat
You to observe this flower, my sweet."
Begged in the name of her true love,
She came as fast as she could move.
2200 Hearing these words, Floire was aware
That his sweetheart was really there.
He leaped out from his hiding-place.
A handsome youth in form and face
2204 He was, in grace and symmetry
Supreme. She knew him instantly.
He knew her too: thus they discover,
He his beloved, she her lover.

2208   Floire, in his love and pity deep
    For Blanchefleur, can not help but weep.
    As they embrace, their kiss impels
    Them to forget everything else.
2212   Their kiss is one of tenderness
    And joy and rapturous happiness,
    And when their lips part, for a while
    They say no word, but gaze and smile.

CLARIS TAKES CHARGE

2216   Claris takes as devoted care
    Of them as of her own welfare;
    She too is gladdened and delighted
    To see them gaily reunited.
2220   Of Blanchefleur laughingly she queried:
    "Friend, do you know this flower? Wearied
    A moment ago, and racked by care,
    You're gleeful now, you walk on air.
2224   You wouldn't give this flower a glance.
    Now there's no thing that could entrance
    You more. Your best friend would be she
    With whom you share your ecstasy."
2228   Said Blanchefleur: "Claris, you see here
    My true love Floire, whom I hold dear."
    And then to Floire in turn: " 'Tis through
    Her gracious help that I have you."
2232   They both thank Claris heartily
    And, weeping, beg her clemency
    And grace, urge her not to betray
    Them, lest some watchman maim or slay
2236   Them. Claris, loyal, true, and kind
    Said: "Dismiss all fear from your mind
    That your presence will be disclosed
    By me. By what I love the most
2240   I swear to shelter you. I swear
    To shield you with as watchful care
    As if myself were in your plight."

This promise filled Floire with delight,
2244   And Blanchefleur to her own room led
Him. There the damsel had a bed
On which it was her wont to lie,
A bed with silken canopy.
2248   They sat down on it to impart
What was closest to each one's heart.

They enlighten each other

And it was Floire who first could voice
His gladness: "Blanchefleur, I rejoice!
2252   Well-spent my pains were to arrive
Here, since I find you are alive!
I have been close to death; I've borne
Burdens for you; I have been forlorn
2256   And wretched since the day I lost
You. I've not rested nor reposed.
Now I have you whom I have sought
So long, my pangs are turned to nought."
2260   Said Blanchefleur: "Are you really Floire
Who went to study at Montoire,
From whom your father wickedly
Stole me away by treachery?
2264   Foolish is he, sweet, who'd assume
That my heart ever has had room
Since then for gladness or delight,
Outside or inside, day or night.
2268   How did you ever make your way
In here? By magic, I dare say.
Dear sweetheart Floire, my eyes perceive
You, but I still can not believe
2272   Them. Friend and sweetheart though you be, *

---

* M. Pelan: "L'humour de ce vers est un peu forcé." I am not sure it
is humor, but the line is puzzling. Scribal error perhaps.

I love you dearly. Come to me."
He came to her. If more was done
The damsel is the only one
2276   Who knows. Afterwards they narrate
Their journeyings disconsolate,
Beginning with the time when they
Were parted, to the present day.
2280   So for a fortnight they dwelt here;
They ate and drank and made good cheer.
Just as their hearts desired they spent
The time, rejoicing and content.
2284   Claris served them faithfully, cared
For them as for herself. They shared
In common all their drink and food
In kindliness and gratitude.
2288   Could this life have endured, no whit
Would they have wished to alter it.
Floire, handsome Floire, and Blanchefleur too
Maintain their love serene and true.

FORTUNE'S FICKLENESS

2292   But in a little time 'twill change,
Because Fortune will disarrange
It, overturn it, demonstrate
That she begrudged their loving state
2296   And wished to bilk them, take them in.
For them she sets her wheel a-spin.
She's raised them to life's very crown
And peak. Now she will hurl them down.
2300   It is her game, her policy,
To cultivate inconstancy.
All are aware that her control
Governs the world; that is her rôle.
2304   None can estimate nor assess
Fortune's extreme capriciousness.
She gives to one, takes what he owns
From another; between prime and nones

2308   Shifts seven times; with indifference
        Treats prowess, beauty, affluence.
        'Tis well known that to simpletons
        She gives realms and dominions;
2312   Rascals get bishoprics, while good
        Clerks beg for bread and livelihood
        Whoever thinks that she is not
        Unstable is an idiot.
2316   Who trusts her liberalities
        Knows not what her love signifies.
        Now she stirs laughter, now brings tears;
        Now gives joy, now gives rage and fears.
2320   Those who are bright and gay one day
        The morrow know grief and dismay.

A CONTRETEMPS

        Claris the prudent and well-born
        Had risen from her couch one morn.
2324   She called to wake Blanchefleur the fair
        Who answered that she would be there.
        Half awake and half somnolent
        She spoke, then back to sleep she went.
2328   The other went to the emir
        Who asked why she whom he held dear
        Was absent, why she stayed away
        From her task at this hour of day.
2332   Claris, essaying to explain
        Said: "Sire, she fell asleep again.
        She read her book all through the night
        So that you might live in delight." *
2336   "Is this true?" said he. "Yes, fair sir."
        "'Tis fine and generous of her.
        This girl deserves to be my wife,
        Since she wants to prolong my life."
2340   The emir, merciful, forbore

---

* The nature of this book is never revealed.

To do or say anything more.
The next morn a like thing occurred.
Claris awakened first and stirred,
2344 Then rose and called to Blanchefleur, saying
That they had too long been delaying.
Said Blanchefleur: "I shall dress, my dear.
I'll be there before you, no fear."
2348 Then in his arms her sweetheart pressed
Her, and she fondly acquiesced:
When they had kissed, they could not keep
Themselves from going back to sleep.
2352 Kissing, they both luxuriate
In joy intense and delicate,
Face touching face, lip touching lip
In exquisite companionship.
2356 With basins Claris went to bring
Fresh water from the pillar-spring.
Returning from her errand, she
Called: "My dear," very quietly.
2360 No answer came: she had no doubt
At all that Blanchefleur had gone out,
So she went to her master's bed.

A SECOND CONTRETEMPS

He asked where Blanchefleur was. He said:
2364 "And why does she not come? 'Twould seem
That she holds me in small esteem."
Claris, nervous and torn by fear,
Replied: "I thought to find her here.
2368 She rose before me. I was wrong
No doubt. She'll be here before long."
Had she supposed Blanchefleur was sound
Asleep, the girl might well have found
2372 Another excuse. The emir then
Mused briefly, called his chamberlain.
"Go straight to Blanchefleur," said he. "Say
She's to come here without delay."

2376   He did not notice Claris where
        She stood, and he climbed up the stair.
        Reaching the stone-paved room on high,
        Through the glass pane he could descry
2380   The bed, and saw 'twas occupied.
        He had the impression that he eyed
        Both Claris and lovely Blanchefleur.
        And why should other thought occur
2384   To him? For there was not a trace
        Of beard or mustache on Floires' face.
        In all the tower there was in truth
        No maiden fairer than this youth.
2388   Seeing their soft dozing caress,
        His heart was filled with tenderness
        And in compassionate surprise
        He went to his lord and spoke thuswise:
2392   "Sire, I have seen a marvel great:
        Never was love so passionate
        As that love which unites Blanchefleur
        To Claris and Claris to her.
2393   Clasped tightly, with nothing between
        Them, they sleep peaceful and serene,
        With mouth to mouth and face to face
        In an affectionate embrace.
2400   I did not have the heart to waken
        Them, lest their peace be rudely shaken."
        In fear and rage the emir turned white:
        A man had stolen his favorite.

FLOIRE IS DISCOVERED

2404   "Fetch me my sword at once!" he said,
        "I'll go and see these two in bed,
        Claris, my boy, a shameless trick
        You've played." He rose, stung to the quick,
2408   Puzzled how to speak or behave.
        None, thought he, would dare be so brave

As love his friend, however high
His rank. The thought drove him well-nigh
2412   Frantic. So up the stairs he wended
His way, by the chamberlain attended.
His right hand gripped his sword as he
Entered the chamber noiselessly.
2416   He had the window opened wide
So that the sun would shine inside.
The lovers, sleeping sweetly, young
And winsome, to each other clung.
2420   No sleepers e'er were fairer sight
To see. Succor them, God of might,
For if Thy aid Thou dost not lend,
Their joy will come to sudden end.
2424   Now that the sun had made its way
Into the room, 'twas bright as day.
The day was well along. He gazed
At them, bewildered and bedazed.
2428   Blanchefleur, his favorite, well he knew,
But to the other had no clue;
Floire, in his dear love's embrace,
Of man showed not the slightest trace:
2432   Upon his face and chin appeared
No sign of mustache or of beard.
There was no damsel lovelier
In all the tower, save Blanchefleur.
2436   The emir knew of none. Said he:
"This, I've no doubt, is jealousy,
Love's poison, which makes one disposed
To foresee what one fears the most."
2440   He bade the chamberlain: "Uncover
For me the bosom of each lover.
We'll see what their nipples disclose,
And then we'll break up their repose."
2444   No sooner did he do this than
'Twas obvious one was a man.
Into such rage the emir flew
He knew not what to say or do.

2448   His first intention was to kill
Them both, his next to wait until
He could find out whence came this lad
Who lay there on the bed unclad.

THE MENACING SWORD

2452   Meanwhile the two awoke, wide-eyed,
Perplexed, confused, and terrified
To see the emir menacing
Them. All aghast and shivering,
2456   Seeing the naked sword that loomed
Above them, they felt themselves doomed.
Floire and Blanchefleur dissolve in tears
As the grim thought of death appears.
2460   The emir addressed Floire: "Explain
Who you are, reckless scatterbrain,
Who penetrate my tower and dare
The couch of Blanchefleur thus to share.
2464   By all the gods to whom I pray,
You'll die, and shamefully, today!
I'll kill you and the whore. Be sure
When you leave here, you'll be past cure."
2468   The two, with piteous wails and cries,
Kept looking in each other's eyes.
Floire spoke up: "My lord, speak not thus.
You ne'er saw thing more gracious.
2472   She's my sweetheart, I am her lover.
I've made a long search to recover
Her." Beseechingly Floire strives
To induce him to spare their lives
2476   Till, with his court present to witness,
He can avenge with fatal fitness
Their crime. He agreed to this, and told them
To dress, ordered two slaves to hold them,
2480   Bind them tight, watch them with a keen
Eye. He gave orders to convene
His lords and barons. They were all

In the city for the festival
2484 To come: the time for the emir
To choose his newest wife was near.

THE TRIAL

They came then, lords of all degrees,
Kings, dukes, counts, vavasours, grandees.
2488 They fill the royal palace where
The crystal pillars gleam and flare.
Huge is the palace, huge and spacious
... ...
Yet it was filled up with the crowd
2492 Noisy, vociferously loud.
The emir's order to keep still
So that he could set forth his will
Was heeded; not a single word
2496 Through all the mighty throng was heard.
Then, rising, he began to speak
In obvious petulance and pique.
"Sirs," said he, "listen now to me,
2500 And when you've heard, speak rightfully.
He who fails rightly to speak out
Shall die, beyond the slightest doubt,
For this would be in violation
2504 Of his most formal obligation.
"Sirs," he continued, "I am sure
You've most of you heard of Blanchefleur,
A maiden whom I bought. I paid
2508 Great store of gold to get this maid
Not three months past. When she was sold
I paid seven times her weight in gold.
Her beauty 'midst the others shone
2512 Resplendent. I set great store on
This girl, and in my tower where
Are seven score maids of beauty rare
I gave her honorable duty
2516 To perform. I esteemed her beauty;
I loved her, found her qualified

In every way to be my bride.
I meant to wed her, I profess,
2520 For her sweet ways and winsomeness.
It was her custom, every day,
To come and serve at my levee.
Yesterday, and today again
2524 I waited for her all in vain.
My chamberlain as messenger
I sent. He found a youth with her.
He took this youth mistakenly
2528 For a girl. He hurried back to me
To tell me: to the room I rushed.
Seeing them, I was wellnigh crushed,
Too shocked to speak. My only thought
2532 Was to destroy them on the spot.
This is truth, sirs, I guarantee.
Then, 'Mercy in God's name!' cried he.
So I thought 'twere best not to smite
2536 Them till they had been judged aright.
You have heard the tale, sirs. Judge the case.
Grant me vengeance for my disgrace."

THE CASE IS PLEADED

One of the kings at the conclave
2540 Spoke first, and this opinion gave:
2540a "Our lord has told his tale. We know
The shame he had to undergo.
But ere we judge, it would appear
To be our duty first to hear
2544 The tale as it is told by them
Before we torture or condemn.
Upon their conduct we should base
Our own just verdict on the case."
2548 The Nubian king, all power and pride,
Don Gaiffier, took the other side.
"Faith, sir king," said he, "I reject
Any judgment to such effect.

2552   If my lord caught them thus betraying
    Him, he'd be justified in slaying
    The couple. Culprits of this sort
    Have no claim to a day in court.
2556   'Tis clear nought can extenuate
    Their guilt, and death should be their fate.
    Let my lord summon them; they've earned
    Their death. Now let them both be burned
2560   I've given my opinion
    And judgment: let justice be done."
    To this view all the lords assent,
    And for the two young folk they sent.
2564   Two slaves held them in custody;
    The youths were weeping piteously
    With eyes of loving tenderness
    Grieving for each other's distress.

EACH ONE ACCEPTS RESPONSIBILITY

2568   Floire said to Blanchefleur: "Oh most dear,
    We've every reason now to fear
    That death, with no respite, is nigh
    To us. This day we're sure to die.
2572   I brought this doom on you, alas,
    My sweet. I brought you to this pass.
    Had I not managed to invade
    The tower, you would not be afraid
2576   Today. Could nature authorize
    Such thing, 'tis I who should die twice,
    Once for myself and once for you:
    To me your hapless plight is due.
2580   Yet, were the emir lenient, I
    Believe you would not have to die.
      And if he really knew the truth
    I think he might be moved to ruth.
2584   But he is harsh and truculent
    And difficult to make relent.
    Sweet, guard your ring with care, and cherish

It; while you have it, you'll not perish."

2588   Blanchefleur replied, sobbing and shaken:
"Beloved Floire, you are mistaken.
Floire my dear, it is I on whom
Falls the dire burden of your doom.

2592   You climbed the tower for my sake.
Save for me, there was nought to make
You come here. Therefore it is true
That I by rights should die for you.

2596   For me, dear one, you stand before
The bar. Your ring I now restore
To you: I would not use its grace
To live while you die in my place."

2600   He swears he'll die before she dies
Even if God wills otherwise.
On hearing her plea thus denied
She brusquely flings the ring aside.

2604   A king, listening to what they say,
With joy picks up the ring straightway.
Thus, hand in hand, and with lament
And tears and sorrow, these two went.

2608   The dread of death upon them weighed
And they were mortally afraid.

A BEAUTIFUL COUPLE

They gazed with glances pitiful
At each other, yet so beautiful

2612   They looked in their utter despair
That no youths ever were more fair.
Paris of Troy or Absalom,
Parthenopeus, Hippomedom,

2616   Leda, her daughter Helen, for
Whom Paris suffered woes galore,
In their best moments were less splendid
Than these two on whom Death impended.

2620   Prince Floire, in budding manhood, showed
A youthful comeliness that glowed.

Although but fourteen, he appears
Of stature far beyond his years.
2624 His dark brows, delicate in cast,
Were of a beauty unsurpassed.
His eyes were big with tears. No one
Would ever tire of gazing on
2628 Them, if they had the slightest glimmer
Of joy. But tears had made them dimmer.
His handsome face had all the seeming
Of the bright sun of morning gleaming.
2632 There was not even the slightest trace
Of beard or mustache on his face.
In a silk blouse the lad was dressed,
A blouse that he'd fastened as best
2636 He could: he had lain unclad and bare
Beside his sweetheart, and as fair
As she. She too had nothing worn.
They await their verdict, all forlorn.
2640 Her legs were straight and trim and round;
No wimple on her head was bound.
Her eyes were bright and clear. In them
Light danced, as in a sparkling gem.
2644 Whether good fate or ill befell
Her, none who looked at her could tell
If she were downcast, otherwise
Than by the tears that filled her eyes.
2648 Her face was rosy-hued and fair
And fresh and sweet beyond compare;
Her nostrils dainty, fine and trim,
The kind an artist's hand would limn;
2652 Her mouth well-formed and delicate,
Nature no finer could create:
No dame nor maid, duchess nor queen,
With lovelier mouth was ever seen.
2656 Her lips, well-rounded, were a pleasure
To kiss, plump lips yet plump with measure.
And her teeth too were a delight
To see, small, close-set, ivory-white.
2660 A man could live and be contented

A whole week on her breath sweet-scented,
And if you kissed her Monday, you
Would feel no hunger all week through.
2664 Likewise, of shapeliness akin
To all the rest were neck and chin:
More white and dainty was her flesh
Than flowering branch with blossoms fresh.
2668 Her body was as exquisite
As if skilled hands had fashioned it.
Her own hands, delicate and trim,
Had shapely fingers, long and slim.

THE PEERS ARE MOVED TO PITY

2672 Not one sage counsellor would dare
Say which of these two was more fair:
Their beauty dazzled one and all
As they came in to the great hall.
2676 No man could be so pitiless
As not to weep at their distress.
They willingly would have reversed
Their condemnation, had they durst.
2680 But the emir, piqued and irate,
Was not at all compassionate.
He has had them judged. They have been found
Guilty. There they are, chained and bound.
2684 In the city, in an open place
Two slaves have set a fire ablaze.
He had them led there, gave the dire
Command to cast them in the fire.
2688 Thus bound, their grim predicament
Made all the noblemen lament,
And most of them, in tenderness
And pity, shed tears of distress,
2692 Regretting the calamitous
Ill star that makes them perish thus.
If they dared, if they could, a handsome
Price they would have paid for ransom.

2696 At this point the king who had found
      The ring the maid cast on the ground,
      His eyes brimming with tears of sheer
      Compassion, went to the emir.
2700 He told him what he'd overheard
      When the two young people conferred;
      The emir gave orders that they
      Draw nigh, to hear what they would say.

THE EMIR QUESTIONS THEM

2704 He questioned them both when they came
      Before him. He asked Floire his name.
      He answered that his name was Floire,
      That he was studying at Montoire
2708 When his Blanchefleur was spirited
      Away. He had found her here, he said.
      "On Blanchefleur's behalf, sire, I swear
      Of my coming she was unaware,
2712 And, may it please your seigneury,
      She thus does not deserve to die.
      Take my life for the two of us:
      This would be just and congruous.
2716 Mine is the culpability.
      'Tis I who ought to die, not she."
      Blanchefleur broke in, troubled and grieved:
      "Sire, this is not to be believed.
2720 I am the cause, the origin,
      The reason, for his breaking in
      The tower. He'd not have climbed here, were
      It not that he longed for Blanchefleur.
2724 I've brought him to his death. I am
      Responsible. I am to blame.
      He is a king's son, come from Spain:
      What woe if he suffered the pain
2728 Of death for me! I ought to die,
      He live, so please your majesty."
      Said Floire: "To her words do not give

A thought. Kill me, let my love live."
2732   Said he: "You'll both die, sure as fate.
And promptly. You'll not have to wait.
I shall avenge myself. I'll take
Your heads off now, make no mistake!"
2736   He took in hand his naked sword.

EACH SEEKS TO BE THE FIRST TO DIE

Blanchefleur stepped rapidly forward
And Floire pulled her back: "I deny
Your right to be the first to die.
2740   I am a man. I'll not permit
You to die first. It is not fit."
Forward he pushed, with his neck taut
For the blow to come. But Blanchefleur caught
2744   His arm, pulled him back, rushed to face
The emir's weapon in his place.
Each of them was intent to shield
The other. Neither one would yield.
2748   All those who saw their suffering
Could not refrain from pitying
Them both. Tears filled the eyes of all
The kings and barons in the hall.
2752   Never did verdict or decree
Stir such a call for clemency.
The emir's mercy too was stirred,
Perhaps because he saw and heard
2756   Each of the two young people vie
With the other for the right to die
First. He was powerless to keep
His heart hard when he saw them weep.
2760   Seeing his fury thus appeased,
The lords attendant were much pleased.

A PLEA FOR GRACE

The king who had picked up their ring
Saw that his rage was faltering.
2764   This is the time to speak, thought he,
For much he wished to set them free.
So to the barons he addressed
Himself: "Sirs, we should do our best
2768   To counsel our lord with the aim
Of adding lustre to his name.
We know, and no one can deny,
That these two youths deserve to die.
2772   If the verdict is carried out
Mercy will be reduced to nought.
Suppose the emir, whose decree
Is law, were moved to clemency,
2776   Providing Floire the tale unfold
Of all he's done, and nought withhold
About the means he used to break
Into the tower for Blanchefleur's sake?
2780   And what will folk say if he slay
Them? Small encomium, I dare say.
If he destroy them, their removal
Will bring much talk and small approval.
2784   It would be better far, I claim,
To learn by what device Floire came
To the high tower, and how he made
His way inside, and with whose aid.
2788   'Twould win the emir much esteem
And would be wiser far, I deem.
When he learns how the trick was done,
He can take due precaution,
2792   And, if he's wise, he will, no doubt."
"This would be noble!" they all shout.

THE EMIR RELENTS

The emir heard their counsel, heeded
What they advised him, and conceded

2796   Pardon, if Floire to the emir
        Would tell the truth, as he held dear
        His life. But Floire made vehement
        Reply: "Ah no! I'll not consent
2800   Unless you will grant like remission
        (Assuming they owe you submission)
        To all who gave me aid, support,
        Advice and help of every sort."
2804   The emir, in a towering
        Furore, said he'd do no such thing.
        For all he'd heeded the advice,
        This he refused to authorize.
2808   And now a bishop rose and voiced *
        His thoughts. The pardon had rejoiced
        Him: "Sir, their death will little profit
        You, since they think but little of it.
2812   Follow the counsel of your lords;
        There's sense and reason in their words,
        I think. For young Floire does not say
        They fall within your rule or sway.
2816   It may rouse their asperity
        If they're not of your seignory.
        But what you can, forgive. And thus
        You'll show yourself magnanimous.
2820   Better to learn the stratagem
        Of these young folk than slaughter them.
        'Twould be a pity, 'twould be wrong
        To kill two youths so fair, so young.
2824   No lovelier could ever Nature
        Form. Their beauty is past measure."
        The cry rose: "'Twere a gracious thing
        To do. Forgive them, noble king."
2828   They cried for grace. The emir heard
        The shout, the oft-repeated word.
        He could not turn a deaf ear. He
        Forgave them with benignity.
2832   The barons thanked him, and his grace

---

* As Pelan observes, a bishop seems out of place in Islam.

And kindness won for him much praise.
Now, amid general approbation,
Young Floire undertook his narration.

FLOIRE TELLS HIS STORY

2836   He spoke in voice so loud and clear
The deafest could not fail to hear.
He told, beginning at their birth,
How they had travelled o'er the earth;
2840   He told the story of their love
And of the ruse used to remove
Her from him, and how, broken-hearted,
From his home-land he had departed
2844   To seek Blanchefleur whom he adored,
His travels on land and shipboard,
And how his host's regard he won,
And how he came to Babylon,
2848   Of the advice that he received,
How the gate-keeper was deceived,
How in the basket he attained
Entry, — they all laughed unrestrained
2852   At this — and, once hauled up the stair,
Was left with Claris unaware.
How he lived, with girls all around him,
Until the time the emir found him.
2856   Then, when his story was complete,
He fell before the emir's feet
And humbly in God's name he prayed
Him to give back his cherished maid;
2860   If he lost her love, he'd prefer
Even death to living without her.

THE EMIR'S FAVOR

The emir was serenely wise;
He asked the nobles for advice.

2864   He took Floire by the hand and placed him
        By his own side, kissed and embraced him,
        Showing him friendship and compassion
        And treating Blanchefleur in like fashion.

2868   Indeed, with supreme courtesy,
        He took Blanchefleur's hand tenderly
        And with his other hand he took
        Floire's hand, and very nobly spoke:

2872   "Your sweetheart I hereby restore
        To you." His gratitude once more
        Floire spoke. At the emir's feet both sank,
        Clasping and kissing them to thank

2876   Him, but he raised the youths united.
        It was his wish that Floire be knighted,
        And for his suite he designated
        His finest and most celebrated

2880   Noblemen. Priam, king of Troy,
        Was never dubbed with such great joy.
        Upon his feet Blanchefleur the fair
        Did spurs of love and gold most rare,

2884   While the emir hung at his belt
        A sword with a bright golden hilt,
        And gave him a cloak many-hued
        Such as no mortal ever viewed.

2888   The fur of it was marmorine, **
        The fabric of a blue marine,
        Broidered with orphrey on each hem,
        You'll never see the like of them.

THE LOVERS ARE WEDDED

2892   As soon as he'd been knighted, they
        Took him to a minster straightway
        And there the emir had him wed

    ** Godefroy says it means a spotted fur. For what it may be worth
I add that the word Marmorina is used by Boccaccio to mean the city of
Verona. (See G. Paris in Romania, XXVIII, p. 439.)

Blanchefleur. And next, Claris was led
2896 Forth, and, persuaded by Blanchefleur,
The emir chose to marry her,
But Blanchefleur made most earnest plea,
Urging by all the gods, — and she
2900 By Floire was heartily supported,
As he in turn begged and exhorted —
That he not take Claris's life
But keep her ever as his wife.
2904 Claris, led to the testing-spring,
Crossed it. Her crossing did not bring
The slightest change in hue or tinge
To the clear stream. It did not change:
2908 As the maid passed, in no wise soiled
It was, but limpid and unroiled.
A leaf from the tree came to rest
Directly on Claris's crest.

CLARIS HAS HER REWARD

2912 The emir then crowned her whom fate
Had chosen thus to designate.
A crown of gold he placed upon
Her head. His treasury held none
2916 More fine. With silver and with gold
He wedded her midst wealth untold,
And at the wedding-feast were all
The great lords of the capital.
2920 The feast revels in exultation,
Gusto and joy and delectation,
With bears and other beasts that dance.
Jongleurs sing with exuberance.
2924 Floire calls his host who had been so kind,
Nor does the porter slip his mind.
Water was called for by the guests:
The chamberlains at their requests
2928 Fetched it. Their hands they washed and dried.
They sat down, with the emir's bride,

Claris, beside him, and Blanchefleur
On the other side, opposite her.
2932 Floire sat beside his loved one: great
Was his delight to contemplate
Her. Carving meat did not deter
Him from openly kissing her.
2936 Mingled with laughter, all about
The palace rose the merry shout:
"Floire, that's the dish you'd better hold
To. It will do you good untold!"

THE FEAST

2940 There was no end of revelry.
The servants all served skillfully.
The butlers poured out the spiced wine
In hanaps made of gold most fine.
2944 In pure gold hanaps, subtly wrought,
White wine and spiced wine were poured out.
They drank, and copiously, all night
And all the gay young chaps got tight.
2948 Whatever game birds you might call
To mind were served there, one and all:
Swans, cranes, and peacocks, and with these
Ostriches, herons, and wild geese,
2952 Fritters and pasties delicate,
Pies filled with live birds animate
The feast, for when one cut the pie
The birds would take wing and would fly
2956 About, and children would pursue
And try to catch them as they flew;
Musicians with their viols played
Sweet melody, tune and roulade.

ILL NEWS FROM HOME

2960 And then ten knights appeared. They sought
Prince Floire. Letters to him they brought.

They approached the emir, and there
Gave him and Floire salute most fair.

2964 His father's death they now reveal
To him, and his mother's sore ordeal:
"Speaking for your most brave and true
Retainers, we must summon you.

2968 Return at once to your own land,
Which waits you. 'Tis yours to command."
Most grief-stricken is Floire to know
His father's death, his mother's woe.

2972 He and the sweetheart he held dear
Turn mournfully to the emir
Craving permission to depart.
He heard their plea with heavy heart.

2976 Said he: "If you will but consent
To stay, you'll have your heart's content.
I'll crown you with a royal crown,
Give you a rich dominion.

2980 A rich dominion you shall hold
And wear a crown of purest gold."
Floire answers that he will not bide
Even though the emir might provide

2984 All the wealth he could crave and more.
The duke came forward to restore
His ring to him. The emir bought
The noble cup that he had brought.

2988 So young prince Floire set forth anew;
They gave him lordly retinue,
While many kissed him with affection
Commending him to God's protection.

2992 Floire's mind was heavy with the thought
Of a father dead, a mother distraught.
Yet he went forth exultantly
For having Blanchefleur's company.

2996 You've heard how he was dispossessed
Of her, how God after long quest
Restored her to him, let him bring
Her home, not without suffering.

3000 He ended his peregrination

In his own land, midst great elation,
Where all the barons sallied forth
To welcome him, in joy and mirth.

FLOIRE EMBRACES AND IMPOSES CHRISTIANITY

3004 His coronet with ornament
Of golden flower they now present
To him, and crown him king, and he
Embraces Christianity.

3008 He had decided, for the sake
Of Blanchefleur, his loved one, to take
The Christian way of life, and thereon
He summoned every lord and baron,

3012 Prayed them to join him and believe
In God our Lord, and to receive
The rite of baptism and profess
His faith in joy and gladsomeness.

3016 Most of the noblemen obey
His wish and are baptised that day.
But after baptising the lords
They took a week to do the hordes

3020 Of churls. Those who would not receive
The rite and, unwilling to believe
In God, his order disobeyed,
Floire had beheaded, burned or flayed.

HAPPINESS FOR ALL

3024 When he had made the land adhere
To God, Floire chose a noble peer,
Rich, well-born, and superior,
Highly skilled in the art of war.

3028 The mother of his Blanchefleur he
Bestowed on this gallant grandee.
What happy destiny this brought
To her, and what triumphant lot!

3032   Fortune, who cast her down into
The depths, exalted her anew.
Her daughter wears a royal crown
While she's a duchess of renown.
3036   She lifts her voice in earnest praise
Of God for His largesse and grace.
Here now concludeth King Floire's story.
May God vouchsafe us all His glory.
3040   And here we leave Floire and Blanchefleur.

BIBLIOGRAPHY

This bibliography is selective rather than exhaustive. The first section contains the standard versions of the French text published since 1850, to which have been added a number of adaptations and translations in various European languages. The second section is composed of critical discussions and analyses.

I.

BEKKER, IMMANUEL: *Flore und Blanceflor,* nach der Uhlandischen Abschrift der Pariser Handschrift, N. 6987, Berlin 1844.

BOEKENOOGEN, G. J.: *De Historie van Floris ende Blancefleur,* Leiden 1903.

BONILLA Y SAN MARTÍN, A.: *La Historia de los dos enamorados Flores y Blancaflor,* Madrid 1916.

BRANDT, C. J.: *Flores og Blanseflor,* Copenhagen 1861.

CRESCINI, VINCENZO: *Il Cantare di Florio e Biancifiore,* Bologna 1889-99. Reviewed by Gaston Paris in Romania, XXVIII (1899), pp. 441 ff.

CROCIONI, GIOVANNI: *Il Cantare di Fiorio e Biancifiore,* Rome 1903.

DIEDERIK VAN ASSENEDE: *Floris ende Blancefloer.* (H. E. Moltzer, ed.) 1879. There are numerous editions of this version.

DUMÉRIL, EDÉLESTAND: *Floire et Blanceflor,* Poèmes du XIIIe siècle, avec une introduction, des notes et un glossaire, Paris 1856.

FARAL, EDMOND: *Le Manuscrit du Fonds Français No. 19,152* de Bibliothèque Nationale Paris 1934. (This contains a photographic reproduction of the MS of *F. and B.*)

FJELSTRUP, AUGUST: *Gotfred af Ghemens Udgaver af Flores og Blanseflor,* Copenhagen 1910.

FLECK, KONRAD: Bruchstücke von *Konrad Flecks Floire und Blanscheflur* nach der handschriften F. und P. herausgegeben von Carl H. Rischen, Heidelberg 1913.

HARTSHORNE, CHARLES HENRY: *Ancient Metrical Tales,* London 1939.

HAUSKNECHT, EMIL: *Floris and Blauncheflur,* Mittelenglisches Gedicht aus dem 13. Jahrhundert, Berlin 1885.

KLEMMING, G. E.: *Flores och Blanzeflor.* Stockholm 1844.

KOLBING, EUGEN (ed.): *Flores saga ok Blankiflur,* Halle 1896.

KRUGER, FELICITAS: *Li Romanz de Floire et Blancheflor,* Romanische Studien, Berlin 1938. Reviewed by W. Wirtz, Medium Aevum, 1939, VIII, p. 225; by E. Gamillscheg, Zeitschrift fur Sprache und Lit., LXII, p. 437;

by G. Lozinski, literaturblatt für Germ. und Rom. Philologie, 1942, p. 39; by M. Wilmotte, Moyen Age, 1940, XL, p. 131.

LAING, DAVID: *A Penni Worth of Witte*, etc., Edinburgh 1857.

LEIGHTON, MRS. (sic): *Mediaeval Legends* (contains *The Sweet and Touching Tale of Fleur and Blanchefleur*,) London 1895.

LUMBY, J. RAWSON: *King Horn, Floriz and Blauncheflur, The Assumption of Our Lady*, reedited from the MSS by George H. McKnight for the Early English Text Society, London 1866 and 1910.

MARCHAND, J.: *La Légende de Floire et Blanchefleur, (renouvellement)*, Paris 1929.

PIERO DA PESCIA: *Florio e Biancifiore* [1490,] reprinted Florence [1600?] and Lucca [1700?].

PELAN, MARGARET: *Floire et Blancheflor*, édition critique avec commentaire; (Publications de la Faculté des Lettres de l'Université de Strasbourg), Paris 1937. Revised edition, Paris 1956. Reviews in Modern Language Notes, pp. 463-65; Neophilologus XLIII, pp. 156-57; French Studies XII, pp. 147-8; Les Lettres Romanes (Louvain), XII, Northern Miscellany (Manchester), LX, p. 3; Studia Neophilologica, XXX; Revue de Philologie, XII, p. 2; Zeitschrift für Romanische Philologie, LXXV, 3/4.

SNORRASON, BRYNJOLF: *Saga af Floris ok Blankiflur*, Copenhagen 1850 (Icelandic).

VINCENT, J.: *L'Histoire amoureuse de Floris et Blanchefleur* s'amye... le tout mis d'Espagnol en François, Paris 1554, reprint Antwerp, 1561.

WIRTZ, W.: *Flore et Blanceflor* nach der Pariser Handschrift 375 (A), Frankfurter Quellen und Forschungen, 1937; reviewed by A. Jeanroy, Romania, XLIII, p. 534; by H. K. Stone, Romanic Rev. XXX, p. 75; by E. Walberg, Stud. Neophil., X, p. 160; by A. Langfor, Neuphil. Mitteilung, 1938, p. 285; by H. Suchier, Litteraturblatt fur Ger. und Rom. Philologie, 1937.

II.

BRUNNER, H.: *Ueber Aucassin et Nicolete*, Cassel 1883 (Dissertation).

COMFORT, WILLIAM WISTAR: *The Saracens in Christian Poetry*, Dublin Review, Vol. 149, pp. 23-48.

DECKER, O. *Flos unde Blankeflos*, Rostock 1913.

DELBOUILLE, MAURICE: *A Propos de la patrie et de la date de Floire et Blanchefleur*, in Mélanges de linguistique et de littérature romanes offerts à Mario Roques, (Paris 1952), IV, 53-99.

ERNST, LORENZ: *Floire und Blantscheflur; Studie zur Vergleichenden Literaturwissenschaft*, Strasbourg 1912.

FALLERSLEBEN, HOFFMAN DE: *Horae Belgicae, (III): Floris ende Blancesfloer door Dideric van Assenede*, Breslau 1836.

FARAL, EDMOND: *Recherches sur les sources latines des contes et romans courtois*, Paris 1913.

GOLTHER, WOLFGANG: *Tristan und Isolde, und Flore und Blanchesflur*, Berlin and Stuttgart 1888-9.

HUET, G.: *Sur l'origine de Floire et Blancheflor, in Romania*, XXVIII, pp. 348-59. *Encore Floire et Blancheflor*, Romania, XXXV, pp. 95-100.

JOHNSTON, O. M. *The Description of the Emir's Orchard in F. and B.*, Zeit. fur rom. Philologie, XXXII, p. 705. *The Emir's Orchard*, Matzke Mem.

Vol., p. 125. *Notes on F. et B.*, Flugel Mem. Vol. *Two Notes on F. et B.*, Zeit. fur Rom. Phil., LV, p. 197.

KLENKE, M. A.: *The Blanchefleur-Perceval Question,* in Romance Philology, VI, pp. 173-78.

LOT-BORODINE, MYRRHA: *Le Roman idyllique au moyen-âge,* Paris 1913.

MOIGNET, G.: *Sur le vers 177 de Floire et Blanchefleur,* in *Romania,* LXXX, p. 254.

PARIS, GASTON: *Les Contes orientaux dans la litt. française,* Paris 1875.

PATCH, M. H. R.: *The Other World according to Descriptions in Mediaeval Literature,* Cambridge (U. S. A.) 1950.

REINHOLD, J.: *Floire et Blancheflor,* Étude de littérature comparée, Paris 1906; *Floire et Blancheflor-Probleme,* Zeitschrift fur Romanischen Philologie, XLII, pp. 686-703; *Quelques remarques sur les Sources de Floire et Blancheflor,* Revue de Philologie française, XIX, pp. 152-175; *Sprachliche Untersuchungen uber Floire et Blancheflor* in Bulletin international de l'Académie des Sciences, Cracow 1915; Chronique au sujet de l'article de G. Huet, Encore Floire et Blanchefloire, Romania, XXXV, pp. 35-36.

SMITH, J. B.: *Karl Flecks Flore und Blanschesflur and the Old Norse* 'Flores Saga of Blankeflur': a stylistic comparison (Manchester University thesis).

SOMMER, EMIL: *Flore und Blanschesflur, eine Erzahlung von Konrad Fleck,* Quadlinburg and Leipzig 1846.

SPARGO, J. W.: *The Basket Incident in Floire et Blancheflor,* Neuphilologische Mitteilung, XXVIII, pp. 69-75; *Vergil the Necromancer,* Cambridge (U.S.A.) 1913.